CHILDHOOD'S HILL

CHILDHOOD'S HILL

Marjorie Wilson

The Linen Press

the story unfolds

Published in the UK by
The Linen Press
6B Mortonhall Road
EDINBURGH
EH9 2HW
www.linenpressbooks.co.uk

First published by The Linen Press, 2006

ISBN 0-9550488-2-6

Typeset and designed by Initial Typesetting Services, Edinburgh
Photographs and art work restored and edited by Cara Forbes
'Mother's Herbarium', 'Honi Soit', and 'One Silk Mitten' photographed by Nye Stenning
Printed and bound by MPG Books Ltd, Bodmin

Contents

Illustrations

Illustrations by Agnes Wilson, The Seventh Sister.
Photographs from the Wilson family's collection and by
Nye Stenning.

CHILDHOOD'S HILL

By: Marjorie Wilson

Illustrated By: Agnes Wilson

Introduction

Perhaps it is because my father's people and my mother's people had their roots in the country. Only a generation or two ago they were farm grieves, country joiners, weavers, tanners, simple folk to whom the sophistication of city life was unknown. Or it may be that, while the majority of our class-mates at school spent summer holidays at fashionable seaside resorts or inland meccas where they and their parents played golf or tennis, we retired to the country to live in a wee but and ben of a cottage or boarded at some humble highland croft. Whatever the reason, we developed a passionate love of solitary places.

During these times we learnt what is sometimes a hard lesson – that companionship is something which, except in isolated cases, cannot be shared with nature. If you would observe the teeming life of glen or moor you must walk quietly, voiceless and with un-hurried movement. Laughter of friends, sudden spontaneous action of children, snufflings of dogs, desirable as these things are, must be left behind.

Of course our love of flowers and of nature was inherited from our mother who would appear in the doorway with her arms full of the forbidden blossoms of the garden – poppies and monkshood and great horse-daisies. Perhaps the flowers, her darlings, in some way replaced the little girls who died before I was born. Three seemed such a lot to lose.

In this memoir I, the Seventh Daughter, have gathered together my recollections of a childhood and a growing up in a time long gone. Sometimes I wonder if I have ever moved on.

I have loved, God knows if wisely,
Every moment since my birth,
More than I have loved my fellows
This indifferent, lovely earth.

'Song of Love'
Elizabeth-Ellen Long

1

A Terror of Leopards

I was born in the very shadow of the hill. In a bedroom to the rear of a dark tenement that smelt of washing cloths. The stone steps leading up were always damp and discouraged childish attempts to mount. Thin legs in white socks. White-socked legs try again, slowly accomplish what had seemed impossible and soon the stair is conquered and the twelve-year passage of your feet wears away minuscule grains of granite, imperceptibly hollowing.

High tenements formed three sides of that gloomy rectangle – the back green – which served as drying space and playground. For short periods on bright days the sun climbed tenement walls and peered down at sheets and blankets and underwear flapping from restraining clothes-lines. For short periods the green was flooded with golden light withdrawn as suddenly as it came. Coarse rye-grass remained harsh blue-green and never ripened or held the warmth of the sun for more than an hour at a time.

The Veterinary College formed the fourth side of the rectangle and was separated from the common green by a high wall of rough harled cement. From behind the wall at all times of the day and

night came cries – sharp sudden cries of pain, the moan of suffering
and the long-drawn-out wail of the broken heart.

Besides the use of the drying green each tenant owned a patch
of sour black earth. Mostly they grew vegetables. Father grew
flowers and along one side of the confining railing of the plot, an
old Ayrshire rose. In May it unfolded pointed buds to creamy
double hearts and a fragrance that made you fill your lungs to
bursting point in an effort to hold it for ever. For you it was the real
end of winter and time to don straw biff in place of the ugly old
velour. For years you carried a weal on the bridge of your nose and
flinched from the sudden sharp blow tilting the hat from behind.

Chiang Yee, the Chinese writer, likens the hill to an elephant.
From some angles it does resemble one – an elephant with trunk
embedded in an old grey town. But for me it was, is and always will
be lion – great tawny jungle cat crouched on its haunches overlooking and dominating the city.

You can't see it from every point, of course, and at one time we
had no view of it from the house we live in now. Until one day they
cut down a tree in the garden opposite. They cut down the tree and
suddenly we had a view of the hill.

It is all lion from this angle. No longer schizophrenic it could be
mistaken for nothing else. We look on to it squarely and watch the
cars and the coach tours pause on the road up. We can see sheep
on the hill too and people climbing up – clambering between its
haunches and on to its back to disappear and reappear again on top
of the lion's head. And in spite of all this coming and going and the
busy ant-like activity the lion crouches there smiling benignly.

Only the colour of the hill changes. According to the time of
day or night or season of the year, chameleon-like the hill assumes
the pearly amethystine quality of early morning or sombre brood-
ing grey of night. Winter scores its rugged gullies white with
snow or frost, and spring with quick green grass which summer
turns tawny like the hide of a Jersey cow – or of a lion.

From the upstairs window we only see one hill but down in the dining-room even with your back to the window you can see the hill reflected faithfully in every detail in the sideboard mirror. So that sitting at tea nobody is debarred from discussing the scene on the hill – the sheep that appears to have got into difficulties or the climbers going up the hard way – and the person at the bottom of the table has no need to swivel his head like a ventriloquist's dummy.

You can see the crags too, leaning backwards, and the Radical Road curving away to the north – earth red – the colour of cave paintings or the Grand Canyon, until the haar gathers itself from the Forth and comes creeping in and the sheep, the climbers and the hill itself are obliterated for days at a time.

I have seen bonfires lit on top of the hill, late at night, crashing through velvety darkness heralding victories, coronations and births of Royal princes in showers of red-gold sparks.

When I was a child we played on its gentler slopes. We walked down towards the great iron gates of the Park past the printing works. Once inside we turned left and climbed upwards on to the first ridge. Black polished rock jutted through short turf where bluebells grew on brittle zigzag stems, each flower a small balloon of pale blue silk stretched on a wire frame. There we played at houses or clambered ceaselessly up and over the polished rocks, nostrils filled with the sickly smell of malt from nearby breweries.

Sometimes we veered to the right when we entered the gates and climbed wide steps to another higher ridge like the Crags in miniature and there you sat nursing your doll in a niche of crumbling red rock, legs dangling over a scaled-down precipice.

If you had stopped by the way for a drink of water at the fountain, the rusty taste of the fettered bell-shaped iron cup lingered on your tongue. A taste soon to be banished by jammy pieces and milk drunk from lemonade bottles.

So the hours of the long sunny afternoon would pass putting our dolls to sleep or wheeling them around in perambulators, here on the ridge where long ago, perhaps in the hours of darkness, some mysterious creature buried seventeen small coffin-shaped boxes each containing a figure. What the purpose of these roughly fashioned figures was is not certain but conjecture has it that they were used for purposes of witchcraft or transference magic. Now we know better since Walter Havernack's search revealed similar little coffins in a ruined house in Lübeck in Germany. The house had been the clubhouse of schooner captains, and as long as the captain was accompanied on board by a little box and kept its occupant warm and washed in wine, no disaster would ever befall his ship; the figure was said to dine with him in his cabin. This was always the practice of seafaring folk who came in at Leith where somebody was either making the trinkets in Edinburgh or importing them. When the church clamped down on such superstition they were hurriedly buried on the slopes of Arthur's Seat in a little cave enclosed by conical pieces of slate. Boys searching for rabbit burrows used the coffins to pelt one another and now only seven remain, macabre and mysterious in a glass case in the Museum of Antiquities in Edinburgh.

You never lose sight of the hill whether returning home from a train journey, or when homeward bound your ship docks in at Leith, or when your bus snakes along the coast road from the east. There the lion sits, dimly glimpsed through smoke or mist, suspended god-like between heaven and earth in mirk or cloud.

Or in the old south side of the town where every street affords a tantalising glimpse of haunch or head and you emerge from the baker's to find his gruff old face smiling and beckoning you to join him in his cloudless sky.

Height 822ft and named for "The Blameless King", people from Holland and the Low Countries turn mad at the sight of him, mad to climb this hill in the midst of a city with its strange animal-cracker jungle shape.

I have climbed the hill on the first day of May, long before there were church services, before groups of students and mobs of the curious started the early morning trek upwards. Jangled awake by the front door bell, sleepy eyed, I joined my companion in that early hour before dawn and looked fearfully over my shoulder at every small whisper of the dawn wind. For this is the first day of May – a time of sacrifice, of frenzied screams and strange religious rites.

Books have been written throughout the years on the gradually diminishing flora and fauna of the hill. Books of geological interest about the basalt and the shale, the lava and sandstone and glaciated crag which make up what remains of this perfect example of a burnt-out volcano. But for me as a child only the memories of bluebells and the aromatic scent of thyme survive. And all that the vast mass thrown up by plutonic forces meant to me then was polished black rock and crumbling sandstone.

When I was a child the leopard hung over the back of the drawing-room sofa. Jackie they called it so that the child would not be afraid – a homely name Jackie. But I *was* afraid, although the leopard hung there steam-rollered and neatly edged with scarlet felt cut with the pinking shears. And every time I put my hand into the gaping jaws between bared yellow fangs I trembled.

A terror of leopards I had then – a child's pleasurable terror.

Strange that my early years should be so dominated by the jungle cats – a leopard with a homely name and the homely humpy shape of childhood's hill.

2

Is It a Smell Like Roses?

You sniffed sharply, once, twice, thrice but it was gone. Time and again you opened your mouth to shout, "There it is! I can smell it again!" But your nostrils held only the rankness of coarse trampled grass.

When Mary asked "But what's it *like?*" you tugged at your sock and thought about it but always the whiff was too swiftly dispersed. So you hunted for your ball and forgot about the smell until the next day.

"Is it a smell like *roses?*" Mary persisted. You shook your head.

June sweltered. Into socks now and shapeless square-necked cotton dresses. By the end of a week we were sniffing the air and the smell lingered.

"Feuch, it's a stink! It's a stink! Stink! Stink!" Mary shrieked. The canary outside a second floor window where its cage hung from a nail on the wall fluttered in sudden fright, shattering its reflection in a blue saucer of water.

There was room and to spare to toss the ball against the wall of the tenement. You could throw it high in the air and turn three times round before catching it on its way down. Or there were skipping ropes – one end tied to the handle of the door for there were only the two of you, one to call the rope and one to skip. Endless regular swishing and curving of rope through the air punctuated by a dull lash against the ground. One, two, three, four, five – and twenty, twenty-five, twenty-six. Monotonous repetition and the dull beat of rubber-soled feet.

Or you could watch the machinists tailor-tacking like mad in the workroom at the rear of the tailor's shop. The big window reached down to ground level but the apprentices, on piece work, never looked up.

The smell held both of you like an unfinished book.

Mary said, "If we could see over the wall I bet we'd see what's *making* the smell."

Finally I climbed the wall. I stood on Mary's shoulders and gripped the top of the wall with my fingertips. Gradually flexing my arms and pulling my weight upwards until biceps stood out like golf balls and as hard, I felt the wall against my body and the toes of my shoes scuffed harled cement. Once I slipped and skin flaked from my knees. Then suddenly I was looking down on the other side.

Now the smell was so thick I wanted to stop breathing. About six feet below on the paved yard an inert mass putrified in the hot sun with worn hooves glinting. Rotting flesh showed blue-black through chestnut hide, robbing it of its vital sheen.

Only the Ayrshire rose could get the stench out of my nostrils. I began to feel strangely out of sorts. At first I thought I had swallowed a hair. "Maybe I've swallowed a hair," I said. Zena knew someone who had swallowed a hair. The hair wound itself round and round the tonsils gripping the victim in slow agonising death. I swallowed nervously and kept running to the drinking tap for water.

Finally the doctor came and swabbed out my throat. He wrapped some cottonwool round a pair of forceps and said, "Now open your mouth and say 'Ah'." The cottonwool had pus on it and the doctor pushed it into a test-tube and sealed it carefully and put it in his bag.

I cried a little, partly with fright and partly at the strange neatness of the hospital bed. There was no pillow and they swabbed out my throat continuously and scolded when I choked and coughed in the nurse's face. The nurse wore a mask.

When I wakened in the night I was so afraid it seemed someone else lay there beside me, not me at all but another being – waiting. Waiting and breathing. The breathing fluttered the sheet but by morning it had stopped and I was alone again.

In the centre of the ward were three cots. Two were empty but in the third I could just make out the doll-like shape of a baby. Once when I wakened in the night, Sister and the doctor were bending over the cot. Suddenly the ward door opened and a woman came in, her face ghastly under the blue nightlight. The doctor murmured something and she stared down at the baby in the cot.

Suddenly she screamed, "That's not my baby! What have you done to my baby?" A mattress creaked, someone sighed in their sleep and a curtain lifted in the dawn wind. Next morning the cot was empty.

One day they sent in a box of wild flowers – cuckoo pint, lady's bedstraw and fluffy purple grasses. All the fragrant wayside things. They had been to the country without me, and this hurt and brought hot tears flooding.

When I came home my knees were great knobs on sticks of legs. My voice sounded strange and hollow and I didn't speak much because I didn't know what to say. At home they were all strangers.

I ran nervously from school following the road that led through to a maze of back streets. High windows of mean little shops were filled with treasures. I bought a lucky potato and found a cheap gilt ring embedded in the chewy mass.

I didn't go straight up to the house. Instead I climbed down the dank stairs that smelt of washing cloths and led to the green. As soon as I set foot on the grass, a window was raised and a voice urgently called my name.

But before I obeyed the voice at the window, I had to find out if it was still there. Uneasy hospital dreams had been coloured by it and in spite of disinfectants and anaesthetics and hospital cooking, the smell had remained trapped in my nostrils.

The tall rank grass had swelled into coarse seed that beat against my knees and adhered to neat black socks. The wall seemed lower. I didn't pause to reason that I had probably grown taller. My fingertips could just grip the top of the wall. I clung there as flat as a limpet against harled cement. Then with every ounce of strength concentrated in my fingertips I pulled myself upwards. I was on top of the wall and looking over. The coping stone dug deeply into my stomach. And there was nothing there!

Where the horse had lain was just concrete swept clean and a strong smell of Lysol and traces of the milky fluid where it hadn't been properly washed away. The Sanitary had been busy. But the horse wasn't there and this new Lysol smell had taken its place.

I fell to the ground in a huddle and picked up my schoolbag. Perhaps I hadn't really seen it at all – the horse. The awful darkness of flesh with bluebottles crawling all over it. Perhaps it had never really been there at all. I had only imagined it.

Suddenly I wanted to get to the voice – the voice that called so urgently from the window. Pigeons were cooing softly to one another from the doo'cot outside the window. I wondered if the old lady upstairs was still complaining about the mess they made and if my brother would really have to get rid of them. I wanted to ask. All at once I wanted to ask a thousand questions.

I passed the low confining railing of the garden plot. There was one late bloom on the Ayrshire rose. A freak thing blooming long after its normal flowering. I buried my face in it and filled lungs to bursting point in an effort to hold the fragrance for ever.

Then I was running. Running to get to the voice. Up to where the voice was waiting.

3

Honi Soit Qui Mal Y Pense

There was a lot of blood. The cut ran from the eye outward. They thought it was the eye at first and there was a lot of fuss. It was nasty falling against one of the great black hoops linking the gymnasium forms together. But once they washed the blood away it was just a deep cut running from the eye outward.

They pulled down the hard brim of the child's straw biff over the pad and the patch of plaster and fixed the elastic firmly under her chin. The shadow of the brim hid the scarlet weal on the bridge of her nose.

Miss Menzies carried the child, a small slight burden resting against her breast with arms clasped about her neck. Little more than a girl herself cut off completely from the society of men. Isolated in a world of women and girls. The same women, different girls. Different girls every year. Thousands and thousands of them. Or so it seemed.

Miss Menzies didn't carry her home of course because that wasn't where Muma was.

She must have thought it strange when you said, "No, not home. Muma's at the shop." The child at a Ladies' College and the mother not at home. That would seem strange indeed.

"You see, I told you," Miss Menzies said brightly. "It's stopped bleeding."

They turned swiftly out of the leafy square. Except on fire drill days when it suddenly filled with a trembling flock of fluttering girls, the square was mostly empty.

Strange how my life was acted out within the shape of a rectangle. The square forming the back green at home; the square of gamekeeper's and gardeners' cottages at Lamancha and the square at school. "The dot beneath the bonnet" you were called then but you were a dot within a circle really. An isolated dot. A circle trying desperately to fit itself into the alien shape of a rectangle.

"Where is the shop? Is it far?"

"Oh, it's not far."

Miss Menzies wondered and kept straight on past the herbal shop with its remedies for this and that – herbal tea, hair restorer, potions for putting on weight and others for taking it off. A strange musky smell pervaded the air. Mother used to send you to the early morning market for musk plants and they were like mimulus or monkey flowers and although mother called them "musk" they never smelt choky-sweet like the herbal shop.

Three red steps led up to the shop and each step had a hollow in the centre worn down by feet that shuffled, feet that ran, feet coming and going over a whole century of time, some still coming and going and some that would never come again.

Timidly Miss Menzies pushed the glass door open a crack. Horrified by the sound of male voices and the smell she closed it again swiftly.

But the child was used to it and, encouraged by her confidence, Miss Menzies pushed her way in looking neither to left nor to right, past spittoons filled with sawdust and worse, past the bar with its ring of staring faces, the roaring fire and the necklace of old men strung around the blaze like ancient beads, all of them smoking pipes and aiming streams of brown saliva at the flames;

beyond the yawning dark of the lift shaft suspended on ropes the thickness of a man's arm and so polished and solid with grease and sweat that they shone like wood. Orders rapped into the gaping cavity. "Four steaks, rare and six cabinet puddings," produced a sound like some giant underground upheaval as the massive ropes were pulled hand over hand, hand over hand again.

But here at last was the office and the mother hastily summoned from a kitchen somewhere underground at the bottom of a flight of perilous wooden stairs.

Having delivered her burden Miss Menzies averts her gaze from the lustful eyes of men lolling on high stools eating hot pies and gravy – "a pie and a pint" – and descends the three worn red steps to fill her lungs with fresh air in place of the food smells, the smoke and even stronger than those, the all-pervading smell of beer.

What would they say at school when she told them? Why should she tell them? After all it had nothing to do with them. But she would, of course.

The mother was quite beautiful with a delicate chiselled face and those enormous eyes. Funny she had thought them dark to begin with but they weren't, they were grey, dark grey: soft and limpid and sweet.

Maybe Miss Menzies wouldn't say anything after all. Oh, but she knew when she got back to the staffroom she wouldn't be able to keep silent.

The child was safe now, sitting on the red-cushioned bench in the office with her short legs stuck out stiffly before her. This was what she loved instead of sitting at table in the long mirrored saloon being waited on by Lizzie or Aggie. Lizzie had a great puff of frizzed dark hair and her high heels stabbed viciously into the linoleum.

Aggie was the plain one. When she married we all went to her wedding and my father wept when she died giving birth to her first baby. They weren't waitresses in the accepted sense.

Muma filled a glass with water from the long curved tap under the bar and Dada stopped putting coppers and silver threepenny pieces into the till that had hollow compartments like huge acorn cups carved out of a solid block of oak, to come and have a look and ease the straw biff from your head without hurting.

Dinner tasted better in here, secure and snug surrounded by so much love and tenderness.

It was a long time later that the mirror on the wall of the toilet downstairs began to trouble you. The Gents was at the back of the saloon but the Ladies was gained by way of steep wooden stairs from the office and approached through a cellar. Usually there was a black jacketed figure in here doing mysterious things like running off beer or topping up barrels or hammering in bungs, and sometimes there would be trickles of beer soaking into sawdust on the floor. There was no door and no securing snib between cellar and toilet, but nobody ever invaded your privacy.

Facing, above a deal table, hung a huge plate-glass mirror and on the mirror in gilt letters were the mysterious words "Honi Soit Qui Mal Y Pense"! You knew the words by heart from saying them over and over again to yourself. "Honi Soit –." Different from the mirror in the saloon which read "Dieu et Mon Droit".

But you weren't to know what "Honi Soit –" meant until much later and by then it was too late.

4

Zeppelin Against the Moon

You could hear the Germans laughing as they nosed over the town above the castle in their great gas-filled fragile monster that was called a Zeppelin. They said you could hear them laughing, anyway, but you weren't so sure nor did you fully understand as the brother carried you through to the dining-room window so that the shape of that menacing shadow, not perceptibly moving but hanging there against the moon, was impressed on your infant mind as surely as the imprint of a negative developed in a darkroom.

Pop-pop went the guns up at the castle but the Germans went on laughing and making their ugly guttural sounds and you crowed in the brother's arms and drifted off to that swift overtaking sleep of the very young. And next morning there was shrapnel in school playgrounds and a baby blown to pieces in its cradle.

Then there you were again not in the brother's arms now but perched on his shoulder marching down the hill from Stirling Castle, you in your white plush coat and hat craning precariously to watch the pleats of his Black Watch kilt kick out above brawny schoolboy knees. Proud little procession with Muma and Dada bringing up the rear and you enjoying indulgent smiles of passers-by and the gallant swing out and in, out and in, of the Black Watch tartan kilt.

And the brother went away and elder sisters kissed "goodbye" at the station along with hundreds of other women and sometimes the men came back but not as they had gone away.

You couldn't imagine what mustard gas looked like although you knew what it did to people and you knew that men used cloths soaked in urine to protect their eyes and faces. But like the sun mustard gas blinded and made men cough their guts out.

The telegram read "gas poisoning" and he was lucky you supposed, in spite of the years of agony and despair, that they managed to save the sight of one eye.

5

Lamancha

I can't go back there now because Lamancha as it was then no longer exists. It's rather like not wanting to see a person when he is dead. There is small comfort certainly to look upon a face, the eyes of which are sealed against the light, the lips tightly clamped upon a voiceless tongue.

Better to remember when trees grew thickly on either side of the drive and woodsmoke curled lazily from the chimney of the little lodge at the gates.

Woodsmoke! That was the first fragrance you were aware of. Smells or odours or perfumes of flowers. Most of us can think of at least one that recalls some association, although difficult to put a name to sometimes.

But let the merest whiff of woodsmoke drift across my path from half a mile away and I stop dead in my tracks and breathe – "Ah – Lamancha!"

To walk through the gates and down the driveway was the first shutting out of the world. The second stage was to walk past the coach-house on the right through the pend, hollow echoing of footsteps sending swallows flickering from clinging mud structures like bats at twilight.

Long before you reached this length though you were aware of the dogs. Gun dogs barking deep and rattling their chains noisily to full length. There was always a Flossie and a Betsy – black retriever and golden spaniel and a liver and white cocker. Then the house dog would come running – a Scotty or a Sky on short sturdy legs, bright eyes peering eagerly from a fringe of hair.

If the coach-house happened to be open you caught sight of the carriage – just a momentary glimpse of the dim shape. An indistinct impression of high delicately spoked wheels, blue soft stuff of button-stitched upholstery and, there again, the smell of an age long past mingling with the fresh bright odour of the present.

You were hardly aware of it in the hurry to pass through the pend. It was there, you knew, a mouldering memorial of gentility waiting to be clambered into and sat down in and driven off to goodness knows what distant parts.

But not just yet.

Now you had gone under the pend's cool tunnel. The swallows were screaming in restless flight and you emerged on the other side.

I suppose it was a very ordinary square. On some estates these cottages and outbuildings are arranged in a circle but this particular little world that elbowed you in was built high on four sides, the fourth remaining partially open where a small secret path skirted a shrubbery and led within awesome sight of the Big House.

For you were not a visitor to the Big House itself. Had that been the case you would have driven, surely you would never have come on foot, you would have continued driving past the pend and rolled up in fine style before the flight of steps that led up to the Great Front Door.

You did none of these things, however, nor would you have wanted to if you could. There were other ways of seeing the Big House. The Big House that was called "The Whim".

The gamekeeper's cottage was my goal and while the Big House would have meant nothing to me without the presence of this cottage, so the cottage would not have been the same without the Big House standing so plain and square and handsome somewhere between the thick woods and the parkland where the loch lay.

Now beyond the pend our backs are to the loft, the wash-house and the laundry and there to the left lies our destination. A tea-rose clambers thickly beside the door to the window above. A pinky peachy double tea-rose reminding me of a Levisca gown my mother used to wear. You would have some of them thrust into your hand as you left, you knew, raindrops clustering the fragrant hearts. Shut your eyes and smell them now, the tea-roses. "Gloire de Dijon" my mother called them.

It was a house where a child was always welcome. Boisterous or shy it made no difference, but for the shy child particularly it was a haven – a place where you need no longer keep your hands behind your back and speak only when you were spoken to.

Down you sat on the padded hearth seat that enclosed the singing log fire in its brass and leather girdle. A kitten was thrust into your arms and perhaps without speaking a word, you waited for the rabbit stew to be ready.

But *she* would speak. She would speak all the time so that there were no silences to make you squirm or questions demanding answers. Just the gay easy flow of her northern tongue as she talked or sang or laughed and the soft fur of the kitten beneath your hand.

There were always snowberries on the dresser – high up – or daffodils according to the time of year. Wild daffodils that were more green than yellow. Slim cool buds from the woods bursting from shrivelled sheaths to small shaggy maturity. Surely they must dizzy the bees with their scent of pollen.

Did rabbit really ever taste so good? Chicken-white flesh in rich game gravy achieving a tenderness and flavour untasted since.

In the act of lifting the fork with its savoury dripping load a knock comes to the door. The gamekeeper swears softly and wipes the gravy from his mouth. His rough Harris jacket, snatched from a chairback, smells of heather and moss and peat and the tobacco thumbed so expertly into his pipe. It is the gentry arranging a shoot.

The meal over, your eyes stray impatiently to the window where the sun pushes in through red blooms and penny leaves of geraniums. Where would you go first? To swing on the great beech boughs and crunch underfoot the thick-strewn mast? It might be you would go to the loch, down the secret path by the shrubbery, looking fearfully towards the Big House windows half expecting to see a figure shake its fist at you.

But first you needs must pay a visit to the stickshed, though this seems superfluous indeed with all the woods around. Still, there is a certain awesome thrill to enter the semi-darkness charged so potently with paraffin and resinous logs and Lysol, surely, for this is the only toilet the cottage knows. In the gloom, with stealthy scratching sound, a golden ferret climbs the netting of his cage to watch, with luminous pinky eyes, a small girl mount the seat.

Then you skip across the square past whining restless dogs and through a door in the wall opposite. There might be some black-currants in the garden here so fat they even burst and spill their seeds upon the leaves below. This is not the beautifully ordered high-walled garden of the Big House with its carefully espaliered pears and vine-shadowed greenhouses. In this smaller garden the podded peas are small and sweet for feasting on.

The baker's van is at the door when you return and you find it hard to choose a cake from such an array of fly cemeteries, made-leines, coconut-iced Duke cakes and German biscuits. In the end you point to the varnished stickiness of an Eccles cake, hardly venturing to call it by the affectionate nickname of 'cheat the belly' because where you come from 'belly' is a rude word. It is a perfectly reasonable name when you think of it because as your teeth sink through delicious puffiness of currant-encrusted pastry, you find the inside empty and full of nothingness.

It is getting late and darkness is falling. The paraffin lamp has been slung on its hook and light streams from the cottage window. Pause as you enter the doorway and savour the strong tobacco smoke. The room is filled with it. With pipesmoke and the sound of music. The gamekeeper is playing the fiddle as he always does in the evening. Sometimes the music is slow and sad – a lament for the dead or a lost love.

Suddenly the tempo quickens and with a few sharp strokes of his bow the tune changes to a reel. On and on and on from one lilting sound to another. Tough open-air fingers are handling the frail instrument with the sensitivity of a master. His long lean face is solemnly intent on the sounds he is making.

But there is a limit to a small girl's day. Already her eyelids are heavy with fresh air. Warm milk and music are as heady to her as a sleeping draught.

She is glad to stumble up to bed for in her dreams tomorrow is here already. The first sound of all will be the scraping of an iron pot and a voice shouting "T-e-u-k, teuk, teuk, teuk, teuk! T-e-u-k, teuk, teuk, teuk, teuk!" and the excited chatting of hens as they come running.

So she sleeps quietly to be ready for another day.

6

Carnival

With a baton my uncle controlled the golden instruments – trumpets and trombones bent so strangely twice upon themselves and the straight uncomplicated shape of the tuba.

He was small and dapper, with a well-cut uniform tied about a slim waist with a broad scarlet sash and a gilt metal fringe dangling from the sash-ends and jiggling in time to military marches and Strauss waltzes. His militariness matched the nautical legend around my cap – H.M.S. *Andromeda*. Having a sea captain in the family hardly warranted a pleated serge skirt and reefer jacket but my mother had a close affinity with the sea, even though once she had almost drowned, and the costume was neat and serviceable.

"Half price for the two little boys, sir," said the man at the turnstile gate, assuming we were wearing bell-bottomed trousers. But father had a pass on account of uncle and we were freely admitted to the clatter and jingle: the hurdy gurdy music and the strange cries; the coconuts and guns; the smell of oil and steam; sweet stickiness of candy floss; performing fleas and fat ladies – all the delights and debaucheries that together made up the lurid unreal world of the carnival.

The lights found us out sitting there so conspicuously in the front row. Hot naked hissing lights that made us squirm and cringe closer in our seats.

The neat figure that is my uncle has already captivated the hearts of three women and resulted in desertion of wife and family. His back is ruler-straight, the eyes under peaked cap transfix us. He is ready although you are not. But he waits, baton raised, meticulously white-gloved hands with little finger poised, waiting for oranges to be peeled, toffee papers unravelled, noses blown and throats cleared until, finally, he has us tamed and conquered. The audience waits on his will, now silent and shamefaced.

White gloved hands descend and the baton strikes the rail of his dais twice – sharply.

But below stage the other prisoners pace and turn and pace and turn measuring out the short familiar confines of a cage. The old male has been at it a long time. His mane, once as proud as a spring aconite is manged and dulled, eyes narrowed and filled with hate. Filled with hate for the man – the man who cracks the whip. Sitting on a box with the female beside him he goes through all the motions of obedience, mounting the box, dismounting the box and mounting again. But let the hated whip approach too closely and the mouth snarls, ragged ruff bristles and the eyes gleam redly. The man makes believe victory but now he holds the whip warily and backs off. The arena is filled with the acrid odour of lion.

Do they really like performing tricks? We're not so sure and welcome the return to the stage of small prancing dogs and cycling monkeys. Somehow there is not the same loss of dignity. The jungle cats make us feel ashamed so that we squirm in our seats again.

And in between each act uncle is there – he must surely have changed his gloves – hands lightly poised on hips, ready to lead our thoughts away from such unpleasant facts as fouled sawdust and wheeled cages of unhappy beasts, into the joyful beat of the military march and the jaunty ballads of the music hall.

7

Christmas – the Leopard Again

We were brought up in such beauty. Not the natural beauty of the countryside which became so much a part of us that it was like the loss of a limb to be without it, even temporarily, but the home itself, filled with rare and lovely things so that we grew to appreciate old seasoned wood and paintings blackened with the passage of many years.

The rest of the year we lived simply but at Christmas three great leaves were inserted into the dining-room table manipulated by an enormous handled key that wound the table apart in the first place then rewound it together again so that the protruding knobs fitted smoothly into matching cavities. There was hardly room then to place the chairs so that people could sit down.

"Gracious God, we have sinned against Thee. . ."

Sometimes the Christmas epergne stood in the centre of a gleaming damask cloth. A pewter epergne with a fine glass plate supported on the backs of three strange legendary animals – or were they birds – piled high with polished apples and pears, grapes and oranges and the flute-shaped pewter vase in the centre trailing with ivy and fir and red-berried holly.

Or father would fashion Cinderella's coach out of cardboard and carefully gouge out the spokes of wheels and fit it out with a tiny battery so that when they switched off the central lights there gleamed the whole magical fairytale equipage.

But shut your eyes firmly " . . . and are unworthy of Thy mercies. . ."

They are waiting for you – the youngest. Waiting for the childish treble. And if you forget the words they cannot lift enormous beaded silver spoons and begin to sup their soup. And the silence cannot be broken. The awful silence waiting for you to remember and to continue saying grace. Somebody shifts uneasily and straightens the napkin at his neck.

"Please make us truly thankful for what we are about to receive." The rest is easy and you romp along joyfully towards release. "For Jesus Christ's sake. Amen." Mother is smiling with head bent over the steaming soup tureen. This time you have not confused the two and started off "Our Father which art in heaven."

A babel of voices breaks out and you sink into merciful oblivion. You do not speak for the rest of the meal, indeed it is doubtful if your voice is heard again during the evening. Now it is the turn of the older girls, one to sing, one to play the piano and the brother to play duets on the violin. And the uncle with the fine voice and the sister who recites "The Hell Gates of Soisson" with such tragic emotion. She has a pile of military buttons and badges hidden away in a drawer and she is thinking of the boys she kissed goodbye at the station and who never came back.

Father passes the box and they break the little gilt bands and cut off the ends in a kind of ritual and suddenly the air is filled with a smell that belongs to Christmas only, the cigar smell that lingers through the house long after the occasion is over, a manly, affluent, never-to-be-forgotten smell.

Jackie is there spread-eagled across the sofa – proud trophy of some unidentified uncle overseas. You wriggle along the sofa so that you can look into the awful golden glaring eyes. Your groping fingers encounter the tongue, a chamois leather tongue contacting the fingers with a soft roughness – a pleasant tactile experience allied to terror. A terror of leopards – a child's pleasurable terror. Dreams were coloured by it and your tongue turned to chamois leather and swelled until it filled your mouth and you choked and wakened, and it was all a dream.

8

The King of Butter

His name was King. To you he was the King of Butter. Between you and this royal personage stood a massive counter of cold mottled marble that sent through your eager pressing body, thinly clad in flimsy summer garments, a mortuary chill.

He regarded you benignly from behind the china dairymaid sitting there on her creepie, milking pail between her knees and dark curls pressed against a fat brown cow. No bathed and powdered, flushed and pomaded royalty lying abed to give audience to his people could beat him for cleanliness. The King's hair was thickly silvered and reminded you of the Silver King, a chimney pot fashioned from aluminium cut in peaks like a crown. The Silver King – King of the Chimney Pots – gleamed gold in noonday sun and red in the darkening of evening but in the moonlight, silver. But the King of Butter, enveloped in his long white apron, also had a silver beard meticulously trimmed into a shape that mother called an imperial.

The King wielded his butter pats with skill. As a preliminary he dabbled them in cold water. Then proceeded to manipulate butter onto the scales a little on here, the removal of a brass weight there until the achievement of perfect balance. The rectangle was golden soft exuding dewy beads of moisture, and the wooden pats left it scored with deep straight lines.

At weekends as a special treat a tiny pat of fresh butter was added to the purchase, small and round and precious, waxen perfect, in the centre of which the King of Butter implanted with deadly accuracy a thistle – or it may have been an acorn.

The King didn't supply us with cream though. Dada took us down to the Dams for that and you went up five stone steps to the little dairy shop. It was a kind of constitutional and Dada liked to see the little girls enjoying his treat. The lady polished two glasses and poured milk newly delivered in great metal canisters from the farm at the back. Then to each half-full glass she added a small measure of cream skimmed from an enormous bowl of milk. As you tilted up the tumbler to drink you could see tiny globules of cream adhering to the sides of the glass and you wished your tongue was long enough to stretch and lick the sides. Perhaps if Dada hadn't been there you might have inserted a finger and wiped the glass clean of every clotted morsel.

But not on Sunday. Not in your white broderie anglaise dress, although you had been known to lick your plate, finding a spoon not quite adequate. But such habits were frowned upon.

In your very early years Sunday walks led always to the cemetery. You, the Seventh Daughter with your sister the Seventh Child walked in front hand in hand, Muma and Dada bringing up the rear. There was only one small cross to commemorate three little girls and no names at all, just initials carved on square stones at either side of the grave.

Marble ivy leaves twined about the cross and you wished it had been one of the plump white doves nestling so contentedly in the arms of placid angels. Sometimes you were allowed to pull a pansy or a floppy old-fashioned daisy head and that made up for the long trudge of two miles on a hot summer Sunday. But there was nothing to cheer us in winter.

Finally Dada put his foot down about visiting the grave because Muma wept so frequently into his pocket handkerchief and had to fasten her veil tightly under the chin so that people wouldn't notice. Or it may have been because we developed so many colds and fevers standing about in the winter chill.

Three seemed such a lot of little girls to lose. They all looked so pretty in the photographs, much prettier than any of us, and you couldn't imagine them lying in white coffins underneath the daisy-studded grass. Cold and pale and still like the little children lying in the wood that Muma used to tell you about:

> Welcome little robin
> With the scarlet breast
> In this wintry weather
> Cold must be your nest
> Hopping o'er the carpet
> Picking up the crumbs
> Robin knows the children
> Welcome when he comes.
>
> Is the story true, robin,
> You were once so good
> To the little orphans
> Sleeping in the wood?
> Did you see them lying
> Cold and pale and still
> And strew leaves about them
> With your little bill?

So the walks to the grave stopped though you the Seventh Daughter and your sister the Seventh Child continued to walk dutifully every Sunday hand in hand in front of Muma and Dada, they together bringing up the rear.

And the marble cross with ivy leaves trailing around it standing in a plot of ground – three square yards lying within the compartment marked 'U' was forgotten and the names of three little girls were mentioned less and less while the life of the family went on until it seemed to be only Muma who grieved for them secretly, suddenly falling silent in the middle of a song. With mother those of us who followed never took the place of those earlier children, the first babies of that ideal marriage and they assumed an ethereal spiritual quality which we, by our very being, our very existence, helped to create and sustain.

9

Sport and the Arts

Mary developed diptheria almost as soon as I came out of hospital and her mother was angry because I was a "contact" although I had only played with her once. Diptheria was a killer then when there was no vaccine and as often as not they cut open the trachea and inserted a breathing tube.

Mary didn't like whites of eggs, tea-leaves which she called "black men" floating in her tea, and gristle in mince. We went to school together when we were five. I sat and waited while she ate her egg and bread and butter finicking, selecting, rejecting.

At home we ate what we got mostly, even the fish I dreaded because of bones. "Never cast upon the floor the crust you cannot eat for many a hungry little child would count it quite a treat," mother said. There were hungry children in those days. We saw them in the streets, barefoot and dirty, trailing after some slatternly drunken mother.

I sat and waited while Mary ate her egg, spooning it delicately from a blue cup, turning down the corners of her mouth and letting out a wail of protest at the merest fleck of white. After egg was wiped from her mouth the rags were unravelled and curls brushed round her mother's fingers, falling about her face in fat shiny sausages tied on top with a poised ribbon bow that sat up like a well-behaved butterfly. Long before I reached school mine had drooped and hung crestfallen from a wisp of hair.

Her grandfather made all sorts of things out of leather – school bags and straps and saddles and harnesses. But mostly saddles and harnesses. Her father was in some way connected with theatrical people and he owned a stable and all the stage horses and ponies were housed there in that entrancing unreal world of St. Leonard's – a world of hot steaming manure, horses chomping at the bit, gold gleaming straw and bales of fragrant hay.

Mary wasn't afraid of anything and sometimes we took a pony out into the Park, leading it by the bridle while it shook its head and showed wicked yellow teeth. Greatly daring we mounted and rode bareback and the little creature would make off with us, tail streaming out behind like Tam o' Shanter's old grey mare.

Her grandfather had a pony and trap and we sat mounted high on narrow wooden seats while he delivered saddles and harness and bridles smelling strongly of newly-tooled leather to farms surrounding the city.

Mary was always leader and I followed in an insignificant sort of way. She seemed to have all the things I lacked – a doll the size of herself, a gleaming new bicycle and the correct weight of tennis racket.

I went to father's bedroom. He sat up in bed in his blue Levisca nightshirt. "A *tennis* racket?" His eyes were incredulous. "You don't go to school to learn to play *tennis*?" But on his next visit to London he brought back a racket, second-hand and with a fishtail handle. It weighed thirteen ounces and was so heavy I could only serve underhand. And continued to do so from choice because it appeared nobody could return this deadly low-pitched service that barely topped the net and foxed them all so that they didn't know whether to stand at the back of the court or well forward. Mary kept her racket in a press.

Inappropriately named "Swift", the bicycle was another misfortune always keeping up with *her* gleaming model on the outward journey so that we were tempted to go on another mile and yet another but as soon as we turned back this was the signal for some fault to develop, so that I limped home on blistered feet supporting the back wheel.

You were left a great deal to your own resources, you and the Seventh Child, having a working mother and father – especially on Saturdays. On weekdays there was school but on Saturdays before you were old enough for tennis and hockey matches, a whole long day stretched out before you waiting to be filled with so many different things all depending on weather and the time of year. In winter there were slides stretching the whole length of mile-long meadow walks shining golden from street lights and a wintry moon. You joined the queue and mingled steaming breath with the unknown, those dimly glimpsed faces, clutching hands and unfamiliar voices filling the night with thuds and yells and laughter till all was obliterated by salt and a glowering policeman.

Sometimes you both waited in a queue at the Cinema, hearts trembling with renewed hope every time the commissionaire shouted "next two", terrified you might be confronted by the awful announcement "House Full" which he sometimes carried out and planted on the pavement like an announcement of doom. You hung about for a while then with other stragglers, not quite convinced and secretly positive that suddenly glass doors would swing open to emit someone and allow you and the Seventh Child to pass through.

But when all was well you walked straight into the strange twilight world of cinema, eyes riveted to a jerking screen and the sound of well-known voices. Sink into a seat and stare upward waiting for titles and cast, a pianist pom-pomming on a tin piano and a girl in frilly apron and cap intoning her wares "Chok-lates, Cig-rettes," "Chok-lates, Cig-rettes" carried on a tray slung from straps around her neck like a pedlar doll. Our nine pennies seldom stretched to purchase anything but you could hear the rustle of silver paper and the sucking sounds of satisfaction. Almost you could taste chunks of coconut ice, turkish delight or smooth rich chocolate. At least it made saliva flow faster until all was forgotten in "The Big Picture" or "The Continued Picture, Episode 5".

If Mary had been with you, you enacted the big scenes during the week – being carried through a fence unconscious or chased by a villain behind the rose bush. Money and sweets in short supply, we gorged ourselves on sticks of rhubarb dipped in a bowl of sugar.

For many years I worshipped an uncle – a younger son banished to America for some misdemeanour – who took us into a shop and demanded "Ahll the kandy you've gaht in the shop." Owing to postwar scarcity this amounted to very little, but we adored him just the same for the magnanimity of his gesture and because he was tall and lean and as handsome as some of our screen heroes.

If no money was forthcoming we stayed at home and painted our faces from the Seventh Child's sacred paintbox. She was five when the infant mistress stared hard at a frieze of fairies all facing to the left like figures in an Egyptian frescoe. "You'll be an artist some day," she said with such conviction that there was no alternative but for the prophecy to come true.

10

The Cats
Froggie and Gerry

Honi Soit. . . Honi Soit Qui Mal y Pense.

I went to the shop for lunch and it must have seemed strange to blazered, gymslipped young ladies swinging books from a strap to see one of their number slink up three worn red steps.

Once the big doors were shut at three o'clock the cats leapt to their places on hardbottomed chairs before the fire which still glowed and sputtered from the saliva of departed old men. As immaculate as diners in evening dress, Froggie and Gerry followed the ruler's movements across the mantelpiece with flickering firelighted eyes, eight paws gathered together in military precision.

All things are one in the cat when she coils like the snake, head to tail in a circle — a closed circle — the symbol of eternity. The unborn human is coiled too so perhaps the barrier is formed even before we make contact with our fellows.

But the cats were not coiled as they sat before me on hard chairs, their eyes changing with the rise and fall in intensity of the flickering flames and the lifting and dropping of the ruler. Topsell the seventeenth century naturalist observed that "the male cat doth vary his eyes with the sunne; for when the sun ariseth the apple of his eye is long; towards noon it is round and at the evening it cannot be seene at all but the whole eye showeth alike." "The apple of his eye!"

The Chinese believed that the size of the pupils of cats' eyes was determined by the height of the sun above the horizon and lifted up their lids to tell the time by them.

Froggie and Gerry suffered no such indignity, at least no more than most pupils. They were apt pupils of the little girl in white blouse and gymslip and if the apple of Gerry's eye should slide ever so slightly sidewise a sharp tap with the ruler on the mantelpiece soon restored order. The ruler's point was the focal point which the cats followed with their eyes – those eyes unblinking like the snake's and that tell the time and the state of the tide; eyes intimately linked with movements of the sun and of the moon; the sacred eye of Bastet the great Cat Goddess herself – talismanic and bringing health and happiness.

11

Under the Pavement

In the kitchen you could stand under the pavement and listen to people walking over your head across an iron grating. It gave you a queer feeling, like being in a vault with the staccato sound of feet hurrying endlessly backwards and forwards this way and that, all going about some kind of business and all unaware of anything that was going on in the kitchen here below.

Sometimes the iron grating was opened and stout barrels bounced gently downwards suspended by ropes from an iron hook like smugglers' spoils being loaded into the hold of a ship. With the grating closed the feet took up their rhythm again – march, march. Tramp, tramp. Silence. Then march, march again echoing through to the very depths of this odorous steaming cauldron of a kitchen where the shop built up its reputation for an endless variety of soups – Julian and Sheep's Head Broth – and specialities like haggis and potted haugh.

You kept out of the way in the kitchen where everything seemed to be happening at once. Mother was undisturbed by the din of unloading barrels and the passing feet where she stood by the table endlessly heaping onto plates the haricot stew, the beef olives and the steak and kidney puddings, adding vegetables and rich brown gravies and garnishes from dozens of tiny pots whose contents bubbled and thickened on a massive iron range to add the last piquant flavour to each savoury dish.

With one assistant who stood ready waiting to whisk away the plates and heap them, under silver covers, onto the lift where they would begin their upward journey hand over hand over hand on the rope the thickness of a man's arm and so polished and solid with grease and sweat that it shone like wood.

It was easy to be at the top at the receiving end of the lift in stiff starched cuffs for serving, but down here piles of dirty dishes had to be unloaded into a huge stone sink before the savoury steaming plates could take their place.

By the time she was married in the drawingroom of Thistle Lodge in Ferry Road mother had already been governess/companion to the children of the proprietor of a well-known hotel in the city, where she was often called upon to arrange flowers or help Fritz lay tables and was not discouraged sometimes from lingering about the kitchens.

But there in the drawingroom in her shepherd tartan suit, her face sad and troubled because of grandfather's death, she listened while father, getting the better of his lack of stature by mounting a stool, from this elevated position swore a solemn vow to grandmother never to allow his wife to set foot in the shop.

It was a vow he never kept which was perhaps as well because mother arrived one day in the middle of lunch hour just as the cook was putting on her hat and preparing to leave for good.

Father was an architectural draughtsman when ambition got the better of him and he bought from his father for a few hundred pounds a rather precarious little restaurant near the Law Courts.

If the cook hadn't walked out when she did and mother hadn't happened to be passing, the business would never have become a favourite eating place and one of the main catering establishments in the city.

For military weddings up at the Castle mother packed into three cabs her staff (some of them hired for the occasion), her baked hams, and her galantines of beef along with ices and flowers and satin damask cloths. Long tables were decked with flags and flowers in the Regimental colours and loaded down with good things like oysters and lobsters, celery and asparagus tips, sorbets and chilled sparkling wines.

About three in the morning the cab came clip-clopping home over the cobbles and set her down at the gate with a laden hamper of left-overs. I wasn't thought of then but the others remember the thrill of being bidden to eat ice cream in the middle of the night.

The shop was the meeting place for judges and advocates, for lawyers and clerks, for shorthand writers and journalists and lunch trays for jurors were carried across to the Courts piping hot and discreetly covered.

Mother could fold snowy damask napkins into slippers and fans, into swans and waterlilies, and she could arrange flowers although she never had a lesson in her life and didn't have to be told to "take twelve daffodils, a piece of chicken wire and four twigs of senecio" as they do now. She had never heard of the distortion of flower arrangement where the tallest daffodil is placed at 'A', a shorter one at 'B' and so on until the whole structure assumes an unbalanced unnatural appearance.

She came in with armfuls of flowers – wild things mostly from the woods which she loved in preference to garden blooms – and she simply bunched them together in a great white jug or a kitchen crock, adjusted one here and there so that they all fell about and settled themselves comfortably into position, and there they shone out from corners and glowed and smiled at everyone so that people paused and wondered how she did it. The house always seemed to be filled with fragrant cowslip balls and primroses and the shop in

43

August was as flamboyant as a harvest field with its poppies and corn and yellow-centred marguerites.

On procession days, when the students dressed up in all the motley of carnival, you were lifted up into the shop window. It was one of the few occasions when you could see, for here you were lifted up over the heads of people in the street, up above the great heavy brass shopfront that announced "Restaurant" which was taken down every night to be cleaned. Normally you stood on tiptoe craning your neck, groaning in the agony of obliterated vision. Always there was a turnip head, a grotesque hat or some wayward hairstyle thwarting and frustrating you.

But in the shop window you were supreme, laughing delightedly as the man with three legs disported himself along the tramlines.

12

Webby and the Voile Dress

Webby's stair was even darker than ours, perched up high some-where along the South Bridge and overlooking the Old Town.

You couldn't see the table for materials, wools and tweed and cottons scattered haphazardly everywhere and hanging over the backs of chairs as well. You tried to stand still while she pinned a frill at your wrist or lifted a shoulder with a line of pins taken from a pincushion which hung on her bosom, making her look as though she had three bosoms.

Mrs Webster didn't look like an artist with her thin grey hair twisted back in a bun and a small dumpy figure, but we thought everything she made was wonderful. After the finished garment was carried home it was hung on a coathanger from the grand-father clock in the kitchen – "Built by Beilby and Hawthorn, Newcastle 1790 – 1802".

I loved the voiles best and they must have been fashionable then for I had two and can still look down and see the delicate lavender at my wrists, the way the frills looked above my knees and the crisp smell of new material. There was a sharp yellow voile too but the lavender I remember best because there is a photograph of me wearing it with, of all incongruities, a white woolly hat with a toorie on the top.

Mother used to make dresses too but these were all cut to one pattern with magyar sleeves so that she could run them up quickly and didn't have to set in sleeves, and I suspect that it was the same pattern she used every winter for my father's soft new flannel undervests.

Although fashions were changing, at school some of the older teachers still wore highboned collars at their throats and severely corseted figures. The influence of a recent war still lingered and we called our singing teacher The German Spy which conjured up all kinds of thrilling possibilities. She made us stand at the piano, hands pressed against our ribs so that we felt our rib cages rise like inflatable cushions, and deflate as we expelled breath through parted lips much more noisily than was necessary.

13

What Has Happened to Eileen?

What has happened to Eileen? The diary is not clear although it is full of it.

Eileen, short of stature, powerful, her head dominating her body with leonine strength and hair leaping from it in a glowing mass of red and golden sparks.

But Eileen has left you for someone else and you write despairingly in the diary, "What has happened to Eileen?"

Eileen's brother catches butterflies at Loch Ranza on the Isle of Arran, and you picture him there striding with long legs over the moor up on the hill above the sea stalking the Painted Ladies and the Peacocks and the Admirals. Not any further. You don't want to know about the sudden swoop of the crippling net and the free and fluttering beauties that have gyrated over land and across an ocean suddenly stultified in a whiff of chloroform and a jar swiftly corked.

Eileen with her red cheeks nipped by the frost, her white teeth and red lips. She has laughed for you for the last time. She has had enough of you. Without a glance she bundles her books together, fastens the strap and without a backward glance off down the stairs and across the Central Hall she goes, her dimples deepening for someone else.

And you are left to linger, solitary. The dot in the circle again.

"But what has happened to Eileen?"

The diary doesn't tell you.

14

Grandfather's Place

Both grandfathers died before you were born. You were not to know the kindly old gentleman who hung oranges, grapes and pears on winter trees for the delight of a small sickly boy, your brother, who had surprised everybody by surviving his birth. Nor indeed the swashbuckling handsome gambler who owned the racehorse Tarabahn and killed himself by colliding with a lamp-post while riding down one of the steep streets over the north side of the town.

It was April when I came to visit grandfather's place – the hottest April day for twenty years.

The road led between wooded banks starred with celandines and windflowers and in the distance elm and birch and larch merged together into a netted mist, black-spotted with colonies of nesting rooks. My mother used to wear a veil spotted black like that over her hat and knotted under her chin.

There was nobody at the gates. With enormous faith they trusted to a printed notice and a letterbox to receive the entrance money. The box was empty judging by the sound my two ten pence pieces made as they dropped. For this was not a weekend or a holiday but an ordinary working day for most people.

A black cat ran from one of the square squat lodges and sped across in front of me. It seemed a good omen and I advanced eagerly. The driveway wound down between rhododendrons and across a bridge that supported four moss-grown stone spheres on its parapet – two on either side. A notice attached to an ancient trunk read "Old larch tree – Europea – planted 1725." A while before my grandfather's time.

But there wasn't a trace of the house. It was as though it had never been. Not a stone or a rooftile or even a fragment of the griffin that had guarded the comings and goings of three hundred years marked the spot where the house had stood.

The view was there of course as it had always been. The hills slept in the April sunshine showing the colours of ancient tartans in their nearness and distance, in the play of light and shadow.

The grounds were well signposted. You wouldn't lose yourself here, not unless you wanted to. I followed a grassy ride marked "the Major's Walk". Daffodils were taking over from snowdrops and the whole great parkland was beginning to tremble and gleam with golden drifts of these flowers. I had only to leave the path to drown in the flowery tide that pressed against me on either side. They had planted millions in my grandfather's time and the bulbs had multiplied and massed together into this waving trumpeting host that met me now on this April day – the hottest April day for twenty years.

This signposting – The Major's Walk – was something new, some kind of communication that had been unnecessary in grand-father's time but today so carefully articulated in case someone mistook the path.

"Please shut the gate" it said, but I couldn't get it open. It refused to budge after I removed the stout iron loop at the top and succeeded in raising the heavy latch. Perhaps it was locked and I wasn't meant to get in. But I couldn't accept that and went on pushing with a kind of breathless panic.

The gate gave quite suddenly, cutting a deep runnel in the grass. I was in the walled garden and only the sundial stood before me, its three steps moss-studded and stained with lichen. "There is nothing more relentless than Time" it read. The dial read five-thirty and the grounds would close at six.

To my left, gates led to the woods again, gates magnificently wrought with borders of black lily leaves, and to my right the tennis courts. All, unlike the house, in their accustomed places all cared for and in impeccable order.

The open door beckoned to me. Of course the greenhouses would be open on such a hot day. The greenhouses yes, but this particular conservatory that was the pride of my grandfather's life, the one with the delicately domed roof and the curved and fluted cornices?

But the door was open and I went in. It was as though the stage was set and waiting. An empty stage with all the props ready, the small cane chairs, the table of blue Delft tiles of legendary animals and birds. And in the centre, growing from its raised bed, the gnarled wisteria writhed and twisted its intertwining grey stems, to crown the whole domed roof with pendulous arching blossoms ranging from palest lavender to deepest purple.

The whitewashed alcove at the rear was set about with Victorian jardinières that trailed and dripped with summer jasmine and camelias and pelargoniums in full bloom. Bumblebees were dizzied with perfume. They stumbled against the glass in their efforts to get in and bumbled in a frenzy to get out.

When my grandfather was joiner-craftsman here, this conservatory was the pride and joy of his whole life.

I stood waiting on the set waiting for the action: for the play to begin.

But the play was over, for grandfather was dead and there was no trace at all of the big house. Only the stout little lodge at the gates remained. The lodge where my father had been born still firmly withstanding the onslaught of winds and rains, snow and the blast of many summer suns. Of anything else no trace, except for the conservatory with its delicately domed roof and the curved and fluted cornices. Blossoms fell all around me soundless and unheeded.

Marjorie
Sciennes Gardens

Sally
Sciennes Gardens

Honi Soit Qui Mal y Pense

Willie

The Big House that was called The Whim

White-painted Ferns on a Garden Seat

Uncle Walter
Auntie Aggie's Husband

Willie, Sally, Isobel and Jackie

Ovinius Davis   SANSORTYPE   16 PRINCES STREET
EDINBURGH.

One of the sisters who died
Eva? Mary? Georgina?

Sally's First Bicycle

Marjorie, age 13

Mother, Father, Willie, Sally and Isobel

Agnes, Sally and Marjorie
The Lavender Voile Dress

Grandfather and Grandmother Wilson
Father's Mother and Father

Grandfather Henderson
Mother's Father

One Silk Mitten

Mother's Herbarium

15

Grandfather and Tarabahn

On account of the grandfather who gambled and owned the thoroughbred 'Tarabahn' my grandmother refused to set sail for Australia with Captain Barker. It was an awkward situation not only because Captain Barker owned the ship but also because in a way he owned grandmother since he was her husband of two or three years' standing.

In spite of all her worldly goods having been packed in a worthy sea-going trunk grandmother set her thin lips firmly together, straightened the severe centre parting that divided her thick black hair and made her choice. An unfortunate one as it turned out for all her name was 'Luckie' for grandfather put his money into an hotel where, for a few years, he managed to maintain his standard of living.

His daughters had a governess, the kitchen boasted a French chef and clientele were conducted to and from the station in what was meant to be a pony and trap but when the combination was composed of a trap and Tarabahn driven by grandfather attended by a flunkey, the whole affair assumed a rather more spirited appearance not greatly relished by those of nervous disposition.

After a few years gambling debts got the better of him and the family quitted the hotel with nothing more than a cracked teapot-stand embossed with a picture of Holyrood palace, a pathetic relic of domesticity which grandmother concealed beneath the voluminous folds of her cape.

The next few years are veiled in mystery so far as grandfather's occupation is concerned but the family found security with a certain Mr Murray, an old bachelor eccentric with rather revolting habits who had been cast off by two pernickety maiden sisters.

So mother came to be born and lived all her girlhood in a town mansion with stone thistles on its roof and a hothouse that yielded great bloomy bunches of grapes. The house was surrounded by fields not far from the sea and one day as the little girl stared from an upstairs bathroom window she was attracted by a large patch of red. Short legs in black button boots soon carried her through the warm sunshine of an August afternoon and shortly her pinafore was filled with flowers, masses of crumpled fragile petals the colour of blood surrounding black shaggy hearts – the poppy flowers she was to love and weep over all her life.

The sea fascinated her too so that one day she set off from Cramond at low tide with the younger children, two in a perambulator and two by the hand, resolutely crossing a spit of sand that separated the mainland from a small island. It was a beautiful day with a salt wind ruffling the baby's curls and beating colour into the children's cheeks.

But the sea betrayed them on the way back and the small party was watched by an excited gesticulating crowd while grandfather's long lean legs covered the threatening shallows and without a word took the small girl into his arms, bundled the others into the perambulator and brought them all safely ashore. His own misdemeanours being so great and so numerous, he never chastised his children and it was not from him that grandmother finally heard of the near tragedy.

The old man, Mr Murray, held his hands behind his back. "Which hand?" he asked and the little girl pointed shyly. Always the one that held the grapes, such a massive bunch with each nodule fitting so perfectly into the next and a neat diagonal cut where the stem had been severed. Until the night of the great storm when the whole glass structure fell about him and he held out not grapes but bloodied hands for grandmother to bind.

Mother was married in the drawingroom of Thistle Lodge – a tragic little ceremony a few days after grandfather and Tarabahn beat out their brains against a lamp-post in the New Town.

16

The Sycamore Tree

When we moved to the new house I was eleven and more like the dot in a circle than ever. I had never been allowed to play in the streets or use public swings although on occasion I had engaged in both pastimes as well as pulling doorbells and beaming high with the best of them. Now these things were unthought-of. I stayed very firmly put in the garden guiding my hoop skilfully with a stick up and down and around the paths as dutifully as my Uncle Major, in a portrait by some undistinguished painter, whipped his top for ever and ever in a velvet suit with a lace collar.

The rowan trees guarded the new house from power of witches and all such evil spirts. Yet the trees seemed in some curious way an omen of evil, hung about as they were with small bird carcasses in varying stages of death and decay, hanging pendant by a leg from a length of cotton. It took a long time to clear the trees of cotton thread traps set by the two small boys of previous owners but after we came the birds feasted freely on rowan berries, for we grudged them nothing.

It was the same with apples – the Ecklinville Seedlings – not good keepers at any time – and you had to be quick before the thrust of birds' beaks turned them brown and useless and spoiled fruit fell to the ground to be infested with fat black slugs. The apple is such a good shape, large and round and satisfying to hold in the palm of the hand into which it fits comfortably like an acorn in its cup. And they had such a good smell, the Ecklinville Seedlings. Instinctively the nostrils widened to catch more fully the nutty fragrance. Autumn afternoons seemed filled with the scent of apples. As did the little room where they were stored, ordinarily a stuffy, dusty place but now fragrant.

The smaller green ones growing on the north side of the tree were firm and perfect but those at the top where the sun caressed them all day were large and ripe and golden, full of juice and sweet on the tongue.

It is good to pull apples. Good to linger amongst the branches with leaf shadows patterning the face. Good to feel the fruit drop, not reluctantly but with relief from the branch that can succour it no longer. Then to place them one upon the other until the basket is full again and must be emptied in the little room that is by this time aching with the smell of apples.

White violas bordered a straight path and these I stood in water and ink and watched them turn purple. We had a swing slung from the hawthorn tree and I climbed up the clothes-poles as we were taught to do in the gym at school, hand over hand over hand with the pole gripped between my knees, and I hung heavily there with head level with the wall overlooking the next door garden.

I thought I had found her there – someone who could have taken Eileen's place, Eileen whom I had lost, but she looked so frail lying on the sofa under the apple trees, pink curled petals falling gently on the rug that sheltered her. It seemed ideal to meet her like that with my eyes on a level with the garden wall but although I visited her several times during her convalescence the barrier was still there and as usual insurmountable.

The old man who was her father called her Dean – "Dean my

daughter and Jean my wife" he said, and you crept away to think about it and sort out the relationship. But she recovered and packed and set off for home and when next you looked over the garden wall she was gone, the sofa disappeared, the red-gold apples already harvested and only the sycamore tree blazed with spatulate leaves and winged baubles looked as though the sun shone even on the dullest day.

It was different with the grownups next door who were all plump and rosy and inviting. You never left home or returned to it but they were at the window waving goodbye or a welcome. Especially Daisy who was fresh and lovely as her name and so full of love for children that you ran to show her your first watch, to tell her when you passed an exam or won a prize, and her arms were always outstretched to embrace you.

She was the sort of person you would like to have been yourself, beloved of children, a kind of Pied Piper of a woman and you visited regularly next door to play bagatelle or to a tea-party where every porcelain cup was different or to play a strange unknown game with a repetitive ritual:

"Who, sir?"

"Not I, sir!"

"Then who, sir?"

"Black Cap, sir!"

And she played the harmonium in the parlour that had French windows opening right out to the sycamore tree which she herself had brought home as a seedling from Kincraigie when she was about my age.

But she turned melancholy in the end and died just when you needed her most. And they all grew old and mother adopted them and every morning she placed three plates of porridge on top of the wall like the three bears, and they called you "the doctor" and you went in to put drops in cataracts, to administer pills and bind up wounds as though they now were the children.

And the old man who was Dean's father still came to stay and told you about "Dean, my daughter and Jean, my wife" until at last there was only one old man left and he came for Christmas dinner and turned green and slid under the table, because he had eaten his Christmas dinner before he came in.

Then at last the strangers called you in and he was lying in bed in the parlour with the sycamore tree casting a shadow and the harmonium silent and so was he because he was dead.

17

One Silk Mitten

If you were an only child or your family had money you might turn up with two. But if you had three sisters and a brother as I had you invariably wore one white cotton glove. Or one silk mitten.

We tore about school from classroom to classroom through the tiled hall, across the gallery, hunting up sisters, cousins, friends, borrowing, cajoling, bargaining:

"Can you lend me . . .?"

"If you lend me. . ."

"Will you *please* lend me . . .?"

Until at last, breathless and hot, self-consciously smoothing the grubby dusty thing on the back of your hand, you arrived in Dancing Class.

You much preferred a mitten to a glove. Waiting to tender your excuse – "I'm sorry, Miss G. I've lost one glove." (How stupid she is not to realise that Alice, pink with guilt and next in line, is wearing the neighbour to yours.) You surreptitiously admire the glow of soft flesh through the cobweb silk of your solitary mitten.

You hold your expanders all the more gracefully – for the mitten's sake. Hastily averting your gaze from one naked schoolgirl hand with its tough palm and badly tended nails, you concentrate on the mittened one – so small, so helpless – in which the wooden handle of the expanders lies awaiting manipulation.

Expanders were a curious contraption of red and blue cotton ruched over elastic, secured at either end with a wooden handle. When not in use you wore them round your waist with the handles twisted together in front.

As the first note struck on the piano you untwisted the handles and held the expanders above your head. Then – "and *one* and *two* and *three* and *four*," intoned Miss G. Slowly and gracefully we moved, throwing out our chests, arms stretching upwards, forwards, sideways and backwards, expanding the expanders to the full extent of their elasticity – "and *five* and *six* and *seven* and *eight*."

Some years later Grecian dancing followed and we postured around the room emulating frescoes on Greek vases. Later still came ballroom dancing. Lucky you were always chosen to be the lady. Only close your eyes and your partner becomes Valentino or Robert Taylor – anyone but the hefty spotty schoolgirl in tight green tunic who cushions you against an over-developed bosom and breathes gustily down your neck.

It was all part of the training to become a "young lady". "A girl is a being who thinks. A lady is one who thinks of others." Ah, but you didn't learn that in Dancing Class. That was Geography, remember?

He stood very straight and still waiting for us to file into the narrow wooden benches. Don't sit down yet, if you do he will shout "Stand up!" And when you stand up he will say "Face east!" "Face west!" "Face south!" Until the room is a mass of squirming twisting girls all giggling and breathing fast.

He stands there surveying you, tall, white-haired and mustachioed, immaculate in black jacket and black and white striped trousers. His eyes are like shadows on icebergs, piercing and blue, like a Viking's really, and he stopped chewing only when he spoke. Was it tobacco or chewing gum or toffee that gave him such endless and unfailing comfort? He was like a baby that has never given up sucking its thumb.

The flower is wilting in his buttonhole.

"Never burn a flower," he said. "Flowers have feelings – same as people. Just let them fade but never burn them." The limp rosebud falls to the wastepaper basket from bony fingers.

"Please can I open the window?"

"Please can I open. . . ?" he imitates the girlish treble. "I expect you can. You look strong enough. What ought you to have said?"

"Please may I open the window?"

"Ah, that's better."

But when exams come round my head is as blank as the contoured map of Australia staring up at me from the desk. "Fill in Brisbane, Adelaide and Melbourne." The map is still blank at the end of two sweating hours and when results come out, marks average 20%.

The last day of summer term and the wooden trestle tables have exchanged their customary daily load of greasy lunch-hour doughnuts for a carnival of flowers. The Court with carved archways leading to the Admiral's kitchen – the original kitchen and courtyard of an early eighteenth century house – is filled with the perfume of roses, sweetpeas, pinks and pansies. Every girl has brought flowers and they are stacked by the teachers – bunches, sprays and bouquets – in jugs and bowls, pitchers and pails.

Classes are over, singing rehearsals finished. Today you will cross the gallery for the last time. They have carried away the nature-study table to make room for the Honourable Members of the Company. As far back as you can remember the table has held a stuffed stoat, a bird's nest and, every spring, the glass bowl with its ditch-bottom trophies of tadpoles and sticklebacks. Year after year after year.

But next term you won't be coming back. Next year you will be beyond reach of stuffed stoats and wild weeds in jam jars. This incredible thought strangles the laughter as it rises in your throat.

"I must come back! Please take me back! I want to come back!" But even as the scream rises you are gathering together your belongings – for the last time.

There is a rush in the corridor outside. Something falls from a slipper bag to be trodden underfoot, a scrap of lace, crumpled, dusty, smelling of gym shoes and its long confinement in a draw-string bag.

Don't bother to pick it up. It has long outlived its usefulness.

18

Mother's Herbarium

Oh, wear it on thy heart, my love
    Still, still a little while.
Sweetness is lingering in its leaves
    Though faded be their smile.
Yet for the sake of what hath been
    Oh! cast it not away
'Twas born to grace a summer scene
    A long bright golden day.

A little while around thee, love
    Its fragrance yet shall cling.
Telling that on thy heart hath lain
    A fair though faded thing.
But not even that warm heart hath power
    To win it back from fate:
Oh! I am like thy broken flower
    Cherished too late, too late.

She began her herbarium in 1893 laboriously and lovingly adding ferns and leaves and flowers from all the places she knew and loved in early girlhood, and even today the small white rose that garlands the verses is quite perfect. A number of verses in the book are signed with her name and she may well have written some of them but here are names of the places all carefully annotated and accompanied by a vine leaf, grasses, skeleton leaves, pansies, roses, poppies and anemones. Thistle Lodge 1894; Granton House October 17th 1893; Sma' Glen; Lochgoilhead; St Andrew Square Gardens.

Sometimes the sprays and blossoms are accompanied by the initials of people she had been with on those outings and some of them conjure up old romances or chance meetings and others illustrate her spirit and the standards she lived by:

> Gentle handed stroke a nettle
> And it stings you for your pains
> Stroke it like a man of mettle
> And it soft as silk remain.

I wonder sometimes if she felt as I so often did, a dot in a circle along with the barriers and the cut-offness? After her early youth, she had little time to make friends. As a young married woman she would carry her babies in her arms to Sciennes Gardens, or in the perambulator shaded from the sun by a confection of a parasol made of finest cream silk covered with frills and minute silk buttons hand-sewn with silk thread. Or perhaps the butterfly blue silk taffeta parasol with the fragrant cherrywood handle that we as children loved to sniff.

The Seventh Child being a tardy error and I the Seventh Daughter being tolerated solely to keep her company we knew nothing of such finery, and mother by this time had little leisure to spare for us. Children were no novelty by the time we arrived and there are no faded sepia likenesses of us on bearskin rugs.

She was what would be unusual then, a working wife, a willing dutiful helpmeet to an ambitious husband, selfless, asking nothing for herself, content only in her ability to keep him happy.

And as she rushed between home and shop keeping one warm and comfortable for her family and in the other organising a staff, cooking, checking silver and overseeing catering accounts, there would be little time for friends and gradually she gave up the effort.

Ships that pass in the night, and speak each other in passing
Only a signal shown, and a distant voice in the darkness
So, on the ocean of life, we pass and speak one another
Only a look and a voice, then darkness again and a silence.

So says the herbarium.

19

Baths in the New House

In the scullery of the new house stood a round stone boiler which fitted snugly into a corner. Mother stoked the fire from a tiny door beneath it and filled the boiler with water and gradually the temperature rose as scarlet flames licked the little door and the water began to boil. Smoke escaped by a strange T-shaped chimney pot that had a swelling in the middle of it and was the colour of a sunset-rose, yellow and burnt sienna. There wasn't another chimney like that boiler chimney anywhere and although the boiler was eventually removed this queer chimney remained as a kind of memorial.

We sat up on the rim of the boiler and squeezed the clothes with our toes – before the water reached anything like boiling point of course. I especially remember the blankets which were soft and squelchy with soap oozing out from between our toes.

Something was wrong with the hot water boiler at the back of a black range in the kitchen and it spat out rust-coloured water into the bath so that we came out dirtier than we went in. Money was scarce so we adopted a hand to hand system with pails and buckets and basins filled from the wash boiler in the scullery, and filled the bath with tepid water that had all kinds of things floating in it – centipedes, earwigs and slaters, boiled it is true but still horrible to deal with. Anyway, breathless and hot and sticky after all the carrying and the climbing of stairs, baths were occasions about which we were not particularly enthusiastic.

Everything had to be scrimped and saved and we would no more have thought of reading in bed than we would have asked for new dancing pumps. Beside Dada removed all the electric light bulbs from their sockets and although the Seventh Child and I tried holding a candle under the bedclothes so that the glow wouldn't shine beneath the door, this was too dangerous to become a habit.

Mother had an ancient blue enamel candlestick with which she groped around in the cellar for coals and she washed dishes and ironed in the scullery in a half twilight that no other woman would have tolerated. But she never complained.

And every so often the front door bell would ring and another antique be delivered – a seventeenth century card table or a canvas measuring six feet by four supposedly of Bruce and the Spider but which was so black with varnish and age we could discern nothing but a few dark shapes.

At first mother would protest, "Oh, but surely that's not for us," but gradually she resigned herself to my father's obsession, sighed and opened the door a little wider, wondering where on earth space would be found in a house that was already bursting at the seams.

20

The Cistern Deity

It was an old house built in 1864 and, originally, long before we came to live in it, it had no bathroom. Then some enthusiastic improver cut a miserly slice measuring 8 ft long 3 ft 10 ins wide and 7 ft 9 ins high off an upstairs bedroom and the bathroom which still exists today came into being.

Mercifully, we were all inclined to dwarfishness. The lavatory seat is bang up against you as you enter; bath and wash basin fit as tightly as pieces of a jigsaw puzzle.

The least that could be expected of it is that it would be snug. On the contrary, around every pipe (and there are many, all bent on their own mysterious business) that enters or leaves by way of the wall is a space into which a small fist can be thrust quite easily. On the stillest day these spaces ensure a generous degree of air-conditioning, but in cold and wintry weather the draughts are vicious.

In the ceiling is a hatch which distributes easterly and northerly gales through its badly fitting seams and somewhere up aloft beyond this hatch lives The Cistern which none of us has ever seen.

Yet in winter, crouching invisibly above us like some mythical monster, The Cistern dominated our lives.

Look to its comforts and all will be well. Neglect it especially during a spell of frost and gradually the volume of water in hot and cold taps lessens ominously and finally peters out. A horrible stillness descends on the house.

Panic strikes. The immersion is switched off, a large fire hastily raked out and we rush to appease the cistern god with offerings. Someone stands on a chair and pushes open the hatch with a stick. A paraffin stove is lit directly underneath so that warmth can filter upwards. Paraffin lamps are snatched from fanlight and staircase where, disguised in red paper, they have been taking part in the Christmas decoration scheme. Candles are lit and set in saucers of water under pipes and on the bathroom shelf. Finally we phone the plumber – just in case.

Of course every plumber is out so in desperation we phone the burgh engineer. Unable after many efforts to get through, we ring Service Difficulties. A sardonic grin makes itself evident, effective if invisible. "No, there's nothing wrong with the line. The burgh engineer's engaged. Afraid you'll just have to take your turn in the queue – half the town's waiting to talk to him."

Two anxious hours later there is a noise like the St Lawrence bursting its banks. Upstairs the cold water tap is having hiccups into the bath. Hot water taps, refusing to take part in this disgusting exhibition, remain aloofly silent. Gradually, however, after much coughing and spluttering and retching, peace is restored and we tackle the dishwashing. The gods are satisfied.

Anxious to help us solve our problems, friends made us a Christmas present of a bathroom heater. I was out when they were admitted – the electrician accompanied by a 3 ft long box. Performing various attitudes of The Twist, and muttering something about joists, on my return the electrician was boring holes in the newly painted eau de nil wall.

The heater was obviously intended for more palatial premises than ours. It might conform to regulations by being out of reach of anyone in the bath but the unfortunate bather was going to be roasted as successfully as a pig on a spit.

We must resort to our old practice of leaving the bathroom door open with a paraffin heater outside and another door, at the bottom of a short flight of steps, closed. It only means shutting off what we are pleased to call a "wing" of the house, and some nasty shocks for unsuspecting guests.

21

Family Doctor

He was an enormous man. I and most of my sisters, even when fully grown, fitted comfortably under his oxter.

The purpose of his first visit to our house was to bring me into the world and from that moment onwards when referring to me he would add, "*She's* one of mine." The others were assisted into the world by his father who arrived for the event, so mother told us, magnificently attired in frockcoat and top hat and driving his carriage and pair. Despite such grandeur he was not above helping himself to a hunk of bread and cheese while awaiting the new arrival.

If you were ill you lay waiting patiently behind the old scrap screen, alternately cheered by pictures of kittens spilling cream on the carpet and children skating or gathering holly or admonished by stern whiskered statesmen like Gladstone or Parnell.

Suddenly you heard him blowing his nose or bawling from the foot of the stairs and shortly your little bay of privacy was invaded. The doctor lowered himself onto the bed, his great weight nearly toppling you out sideways.

He talked of everything – the weather, some incident he had seen in the street, books or pictures, of everything excepting you and your sore throat and the fact that you were running a temperature. All this was part of that long-dead accomplishment – the art of diagnosis. While you attempted to respond he was taking your pulse, fixing a thermometer under your armpit, watching your eyes, your breathing, and observing you closely.

Then came the solemn moment when he pronounced the name of the ailment and prescribed medicine. "And don't dare move from that bed till I come back, d'you hear?"

Now was the time to produce the box. It had been a present from an old patient and in it he kept the loose tobacco which he rolled up into untidy cigarettes. The doctor was a keen fisherman and the lid was tastefully decorated with a fishing fly as well as the words The Doctor. However when the lid was opened there was another fly on the underside called The Bloody Butcher. Ask any fisherman and he will confirm that these are two authentic fishing flies.

The tobacco was loosely placed on a square of fine paper. Rolling it backwards and forwards he eventually produced a roughly cylindrical shape and this was held together by licking the gummed edge with his tongue. Any escaping wisps of tobacco were carefully swept off the bed and into the box.

He went out leaving behind him a brief spiral of smoke, the smell of tweeds, of good soap and the out-of-doors. Downstairs he donned the greatcoat inherited from his father along with pearl pin and cravat. When helping him on with this coat it was difficult to lift it above the level of his waist.

When my sister was expecting her baby he began the tedious climb to her fourth-floor flat. As he mounted the last flight he boomed out, "Is God in?"

Visiting at his house was quite different. At one time we were allowed to wait in the elegant dining-room but, latterly, we sat around the entrance hall. Our feet sank in rich carpeting, delicious odours of a recently-served meal drifted up from the basement and we occupied our waiting time by examining the prized prints, engravings and etchings which hung the walls from the front door, along the whole length of hall on both sides and disappeared down the long red-carpeted staircase to the basement.

Never a visiting hour passed but there was an "incident". In order that he might hear the doorbell the door of his consulting room was left standing slightly open. He was quite unaware, I think, that the result was sometimes embarrassing and highly entertaining – to those outside.

One evening a douce wee body in black was called in and we heard the usual murmur of question and answer. Suddenly we were startled to hear his booming voice,

"Right, Mrs X. Up with your shirty."

Another night it was the turn of a very attractive young woman.

"Well, what's this you've been up to? You've been eating broth, woman – great plates of broth with peas and veges. Your stomach's full of wind, that's what's wrong with you."

No use being sorry for yourself.

"Tired? Well, who's not tired these days?" he would roar. And, stooping to lift something off the floor, he would accompany the action with such groanings and moanings and clutchings of his back you felt that he should be the patient and your ailments paled into insignificance.

Then there were the occasions when the first editions were produced from the glass-fronted bookcase in his consulting room. Holding them reverently you sat on the black horsehair sofa while he explained why the cut of the paper or the printing on the fly-leaf distinguished this from any other copy.

Once in the middle of a dull session as he was showing a patient out, a little man walked in clutching an engraving under his arm. He whispered in the doctor's ear.

"A Morley? Do you think so?" The doctor examined the picture closely. "You know, it might be. Look at that hand."

Off he went to get his magnifying glass and there followed a tour round every Morley in the hall. Suddenly he paused and looked around his patients who were certainly living up to the name.

"Ah," he shouted, "we'll hear what the expert's got to say – AGNES!"

And the Seventh Child who knew something about art was pressed into service.

Nowadays a visit to the doctor has no such entertaining sidelines. As you go in you lift a numbered card from a pile on the hall table. When your turn comes the doctor pops his head round the door and calls the number, rather like the old game of Postman's Knock. The visit is short and to the point – the doctor is a busy man.

But how you miss the reassuring hand on your shoulder as you leave and the booming voice:

"Give my love to Mothery!"

22

Black Patent Shoes

You wanted to go on wearing the black patent and light kid shoes for ever. The straps buttoned over the bridge of your foot and you only got to wear them on Sundays. And each Sunday it seemed the buttonhook tugged harder and harder to bring the buttons into place. But you wouldn't let the pain show on your face as it pinched the skin because when that happened you had outgrown them and it would be the boots again.

How you hated the boots! You wore them all summer at the cottage and they sucked your socks greedily down into their black depths. No amount of pulling up ever made them stay. Within five minutes they were under the soles of the feet again so that you limped to avoid the lumps.

But the shoes – they were worn with the black satin coat and bonnet – the bonnet with rosebuds framing the face. Father stood you up on the church pew and the pages of the hymnary were as fine as rice paper whiffling through your fingers.

There was no finery at the rented cottage. With the boots you wore a coarse natural linen dress that had a scarlet belt somewhere about the region of the thighs.

The Howgate road was quiet in those days with nothing much more than a hay wagon to set the dust dancing so that you could draw a face with a forefinger on the toes of the boots. We drew water from a well across the road and it splashed from full pails to trace runnels in the dust. The well was fern-shaded and cool and spiders scuttled across its surface like mechanical creatures from a Magic Shop. You would lean down and cup the spring water in your hands and listen to it drip, dripping somewhere away in the darkness.

If you came to the cottage in winter or early spring the roads and the dykes were filled with snow. So white and so silent and so deep you had to be carried and it had to be dug away from gate and path and roadway. It couldn't have been so very deep either because in the morning snowdrops had pierced the surface and the air was filled with the smell of it melting. Then there was the pain of small cold hands and the agony of having them plunged into hot water and feeling frozen blood surge too quickly and too insistently against the fingertips.

The first time you went to Foley's Farm was for a birthday party. On the way you passed Mrs Pow of the "Walltower". It was impossible to reach the farm without passing her because Mrs Pow was always there, a strange mysterious figure in black peering out at you from the hollies and the firs and the junipers that crowded about her gloomy mansion house. You went with quickened steps then for, in company with the Foley children, you were guilty of stealing small hard apples from her orchard.

The party was held outside and as Foley's Farm was a pig farm you wore the linen dress with the red belt and, of course, the boots. There was no birthday cake but there was an enormous bowl of curds and a jug full of thick yellow cream. When the bowl was empty David, the eldest Foley boy, smoked a nest of bumblebees and dug out a comb of rich wild honey. It wasn't very clean but it tasted of pansies and pinks and peonies and you held up your mouth to catch it as it dripped off the thick bread. You always thought these were the same bees that bumbled companionably all through the night in the wall above the old box bed and you were sorry you had eaten the honey.

There were always willow trees in the sparse little wood at the cross roads. The willows stood with feet planted in a bog and in spring the peaty bog water trembled into life as tadpoles hatched from jellied spawn and pussy willows turned from soft grey to great pollen balls of golden yellow. All day the sound of honey bees was as rhythmic as the humming of telegraph poles until the sun passed from the wood and the plundered trees stood silent.

The road stretched between high sloping banks where bluebells and small quivering butterflies were scarcely distinguishable one from another and on Sundays especially, it was so still you could hear the hot shimmering air rake through the wild flowers and the shaker grasses. Then the cackling of a hen boastful of the speckled egg she had just laid would set you thinking of tea and down you ran on to the road again.

Sometimes about midnight a voice would waken you – a voice singing in the darkness – "I'm Georgie R-R-R-Rickaby. What do you think of me?" It was father walking up from Penicuik and scaring away shadows that lurked behind every tree between Pomathorn and the crossroads. He sang mostly for company not because he was scared because father was never afraid of anything.

Nowadays a grand new house dominates the cottage. Then it was the ash tree. In summer there was hardly a day or an hour or a minute without some stray breath of air setting up whisperings amongst the leaves and in winter or March gales, the swayings and crashings of black branches caused a crepitus of sound. The sound wakened you out of sleep – or it might be a cow with her horns entangled as she scratched her neck on the wire fence.

The field at the back sloped down to a burn. You didn't know the name of the burn or where it came from or even where it went to after it left the field. Down the field you went headlong, scattering nesting larks as you ran, cuckoospit from ladies' smocks spattering your legs with froth. The hated boots were flung upon the bank and toes wriggled in delicious company with sticklebacks and darting minnows.

You didn't go to Foley's Farm for milk. Instead you walked down in the opposite direction towards the village, stopping to run down a lane and bury your nose in fragrant lilac spikes that hung heavy over the Manse wall.

Milk was sold at the Robertson's Farm in metal cans with a handle – warm and topped by creamy froth. Sometimes you got to hold the cow's tail so that it didn't lash out as Mrs. Robertson leant her rosy face against its side. You stood silently there in the byre's half-twilight listening to the rhythmic hissing of milk in the pail.

There the sounds of the byre were created for you for all time – the sudden alarm of rattling chains as a brown triangular head turned to regard you with gentle eyes 'so thickly lashed against the summer sun', stamping of hooves, spattering of dung, chewing of cud and contented expulsion of warm sweet clover-scented breath. Above all, the smell and the sound of spurting milk.

People say you are in your dotage if you dwell too much in the past. Of course all good things didn't happen in childhood. I remember once at a picnic, having eaten all the food, drunk all the lemonade, made tea twice on a wood fire and played all the games, we discovered it was still only midday. It seemed all the good things were over and there was nothing left. Life would be unbearable then if all the good things had been experienced by midday with afternoon and evening yet to come.

Meantime summer is over at the cottage and you go back to the city – back to the black satin coat and bonnet and, if you are lucky, you find that the round black buttons of the cherished shoes can still be coaxed no matter how unwillingly into the buttonholes.

23

Rab and His Friends

There were two roads you could take to Howgate in those days and Liberton Brae was the starting point for both of them unless you were approaching by Swanston and Hillend when you joined the road beyond Straiton. Both roads I'm thinking of crossed Roslin Moor and the first wound down the steep hill to the village of Auchendinny following the direction taken by James Noble, the Howgate carter, on that last fateful journey with Jess steaming between the shafts and Ailie happed carefully "in two pairs of clean old blankets having at their corners A.G. 1794 in large letters in red worsted". As the story goes, Ailie lying on the floor of the cart with her beautiful sealed face open to the heavens and Rab taking up his usual position behind. Dr. John Brown heard the solitary cart echoing over the cobbles of Nicolson Street "and die away and come again".

So taking that road you would pass down the hill through Auchendinny woods past haunted Woodhouselee and so on to Howgate itself, where Rab is buried in the braeface beside the burn with village children "who used to make very free with him and sit on his ample stomach as he lay half asleep at the door in the sun, watching the solemnity."

We were brought up on "Rab and his Friends" immortalising as it did the village of Howgate which was a stage on the old road between Peebles and Edinburgh. About the year 1806 a post-chaise called The Fly used to halt there for one hour on its five hour journey from Peebles to Edinburgh.

But in our time there was no post-chaise, no bus even passing through this moorland village situated 800 feet above sea level, and the old coaching inn was little more than a village pub standing as it did in the shadow of four great ash trees. So we walked up from Penicuik itself having survived the bus journey up Liberton Brae which seemed so steep then and the vehicle's mechanics so inadequate that it stopped and jerked and coughed in an agony of effort and I sat tense and fearfully waiting for its inevitable plunge backwards downhill. But it never happened. Somehow we reached the top, be the ascent ever so slow and difficult and I leant forwards to add my slight weight to its final triumphal surge up and over the top.

The road from Penicuik wound steeply down between cottages on the left and a high green bank on the right. At the top of this righthand incline, secured, we fervently hoped, behind adequate fencing, bellowed a huge black bull. He not only made himself heard, he followed our passing, perched perilously and menacing above us, through the narrow gorge that held the river in its hollow.

But as we climbed the hill towards Pomathorn his domain appeared to be further shut off and he was gradually left behind, and our attention became absorbed by the gorge on the left and the thrilling approach to the Level Crossing. On rare occasions the gates were closed and we arrived breathless just in time to see the sparks and feel the ground thunder under our feet. But mostly the gates were open and there was nothing in the quiet country road other than a collie dog or a few cackling hens.

It was a far cry uphill though for two small girls and worse for the grownups who carried provisions and luggage for perhaps a week's stay. Our visitors must really have wanted to visit us for there was always someone at weekends toiling up to the cross-roads and coming in at the cottage gate between rows of pansies, the gooseberries and the blackcurrants, and at dinner there would be potatoes father had grown – white and mealy and bursting like froth from their skins.

Danny used to come out a lot – Danny the butcher with a cloth cap on his head and rolls of fat at the back of his neck. He supplied the shop with meat and he gave me sugar lumps to suck when I thought I had swallowed a hair and mother said he saved the brother's life with juicy hot marrow scooped from hollow bones and eaten mixed with oatmeal spread on hot buttered toast.

I had mumps at the cottage and felt strange and peculiar running around with lumps on my neck and swathed in a white woollen shawl.

Sometimes we went to the seaside for holidays and took a house in Dunbar for a month, and you and the Seventh Child caught baby flounders in shallow sun-warmed water under the bridge at Belhaven sands. And you bathed sometimes in the swimming pool and sometimes in the sea itself and you wore a shepherd tartan bathing cap that had long since perished so that small flakes of rubber came off on your hands and onto your hair and the older sisters thrust shivery bites between your teeth to keep them from chittering.

Your cap had perished and had a peculiar old rubbery smell but the elder sisters had caps with frills round them and they lay about gracefully on rocks with beach shoes laced Grecian fashion right up to their knees.

And the house was called "Abbeylands" and there was a harmonium in the parlour and a little maid who kept announcing, "please, mum, the matches is finished."

But you liked the cottage best and years later you cried about Ailie and about John Noble the Howgate carter but mostly about Rab who had to be brained with a rack pin "for there was nae doin' wi' him" once his master and mistress were dead and he was taken over by the new carter.

24

The Night Fliers

While most people were getting married and settling down thereby ensuring that they had a husband in their bedrooms I was contentedly trapping in jam jars the night fliers – those heavy-winged creatures that invade our homes of a summer's evening. The night fliers which all night long flutter and poise and pursue their love lives amongst ghost flowers of summer jasmine and dusky blooms of stocks until lights flickering one by one from open windows decoy them from their purpose.

Regarded by most with at the very least annoyance and by some with actual revulsion, the night moths, turned to crazed blundering creatures by the naked scorching brilliance of one hundred watt bulbs which to these soft velvety bodies must surely ape the sun, generally meet abrupt and sudden dispatch at the end of a folded newspaper.

Which is a pity for while to the naked eye they appear hideous and menacing with a horrible tendency to entangle themselves in human hair and even penetrate the bedclothes, looked at under a magnifying lens even the uniformly grey Gothic moth is transformed into a creature whose dark shining wings, covered with a network of golden lace, carry like some stamp of aerial perfection the Gothic arches from which it derives its name.

The Underwings both red and yellow appear similarly heavy-bodied and dull until in a moment of sudden flight you glimpse the brilliant colour bordered by black so skilfully concealed by nondescript upper wings which prevent birds butchering the bodies and discarding delicate paper-fine wings.

Far more interesting than the Grey Dagger moth itself which carries four black daggers like a menace on its forewings is the caterpillar, so improbably fashioned as to outdo any of those grotesque malformed monsters, sometimes barely human, which once made sport for kings.

I came upon a Grey Dagger caterpillar and almost grasped it one mellow September day when mother and I were in the garden pulling and preparing pears for bottling. It was a race who should get the pears first – ourselves or the birds. Even our presence did nothing to scare them off and they just sat there – blackbirds and starlings mostly – beaks stabbing into the luscious sweetness leaving the ground strewn with well-picked cores.

This one and a half inch of caterpillar is black with a yellow stripe running down the centre of its back, the black area liberally spotted with scarlet and a further stripe of white that merges finally into grey beneath. On the fourth segment a large raised tubercle resembles a black horn, and on the eleventh there is a smaller warty protuberance. And all this magnificence is covered with silky sable hair, a tuft of which stands straight up on the rear protuberance like a tail finished off with a yellow spot of a full stop. This punctuation mark is of course merely a continuation of the yellow stripe along its back.

Why this fantastic make-up for a caterpillar which people rarely see and would not ponder over for a moment even if they did? And this during only one metamorphosis of egg to caterpillar, caterpillar to chrysalis and finally chrysalis to seemingly dull and heavy insignificance.

As we sat in the sun peeling and coring the pears for bottling she in her pale blue linen kirtled about her waist so that she resembled some classical goddess busied at a festival – for she had a way without any effort on her part at all of making herself look different – we were part of a scene of great activity. The birds continued to attack the remaining fruit with gusto. Wasps buzzed around discarded peelings or lay like drunken infants sucking in the sweetness that dripped from our knives. Sometimes in occasional skirmish honeybees chased the wasps and took possession but in the main they left one another alone. There was more than enough for all.

Most moths are night fliers sleeping and very sensibly tucked out of sight during daylight hours but the few who behave like butter-flies enjoy flying in the sunshine or alighting on flowers to rest in its warmth. Among this minority is the Burnet moth endeared to us by a sluggish habit in the mornings which earns it the name of "the ten o'clock sleeper". This and clubbed antennae distinguish the Burnet moths – the five and six-spot and the Burnet Companion – from all other moths.

I came on them once in Skye – a community of six-spot Burnets halfway down a cliff in a small quivering marshy plateau which held in a radiant shimmer of colour ragged robin, meadow-sweet, clovers and buttercups, thistles and knapweeds. Here on knapweeds in a drugged and noonday sleep clung the Burnets – not one or two but dozens of these gorgeous gregarious creatures – long silken blue-black wings spotted with scarlet and blending with the crimson and purple of their host flowers in breathtaking marriage.

So deep was their slumber it was even possible to pluck a knap-weed and carry it not only to the farmhouse but back again to the flower-studded hollow without disturbing the moth.

The Garden Tiger rested on a stone amongst pink flowers of sea milkwort on the shores of Loch Torridon. It rested with wings folded and sloping like the eaves of a house and the reddish-orange underwings spotted with round black or indigo-blue spots were hidden. Even so, with its cream and brown forewings, furry dark brown thorax, orange-red abdomen with black bars and the white of thread-like antennae, it was magnificent.

This Tiger has a "Woolly Bear" caterpillar covered with long black and sable hairs which used to be regarded with fear by country folk. Should the caterpillar succeed in coiling itself round your finger you would never get it off and would waste away, and because the same superstition persisted in France it had the name "Anneau du Diable".

The moths. The night fliers. Not the children I might have had perhaps but they filled a place and a purpose and they kept me content.

25

All of One Frosty Day

The commotion started as first light began to strengthen in the east. On a morning of frosty stillness such as this the only birdsong usually to be heard was the hopeful chirruping of robin or blackbird hopping expectantly around the bird table.

But this day the clamour was tremendous so that as soon as breakfast was over I made my way out to the garden. It wasn't that great hunter the ginger tom lurking beneath the hawthorn tree dangling his limp and feathered prey, and for some time I could see nothing to account for the disturbance.

At last I spotted him perched on a low branch of the apple tree so that by stretching upwards I could almost have touched him – a tawny owl immobilised by daylight. The tree was full of birds hysterical in their scolding – blackbirds, mavis, sparrow, starling and venturing closer than any, the blue tits.

Unmoved, the enemy sat stolidly while the sun climbed in the sky and the apple tree's shadow grew shorter on the hoary earth, disappeared altogether then lengthened slowly across the grass.

At intervals during the day I spoke to him and he turned his head with such slow smooth grace and a blink of sleepy golden eyes. All day the birds mobbed him except when they appeased their hunger.

Towards the close of the winter afternoon when the frosty sun resembled a great blood orange he took wing silently and mysteriously and so ended a long day's vigil in a city garden.

And that was a strange thing for not long afterwards I was weeding under that apple tree and the spade turned up a blue stone, a turquoise – a most beautiful shade of blue like the sky and with unusual markings. Oval-shaped and convex, it looked as though it might once have been set in a ring.

I didn't throw it away because I liked it, just as I love the legends and folklore that have grown up around the turquoise. What was even stranger was that next day, when the Seventh Child was lifting away the weeds which I, in my indolence, had left lying, she picked up what turned out to be the setting for the stone. It was an owl with turquoise eyes and blue enamelled wings and an oval space into which my stone fitted perfectly.

Had the owl petrified with cold and fallen to the earth or had the gods turned him to metal and enamel and toppled him from his perch? I had hoped the metal might be gold because no one had owned such a brooch while we lived in the house which was a very long time indeed and it didn't seem possible that any baser metal could survive such long interment in the soil. But base metal it was, the testing acid bubbling and turning to verdi gris when it made contact.

It seemed such a coincidence that the two separate parts of the brooch, the breathtakingly blue turquoise and its charming setting making up the main structure of the owl's body should come together at last, not found on the same day even and so narrowly missing the sack of garden rubbish.

It makes no difference, not being gold I mean. It is still an exquisite thing with delicately pointed ears, feathered wings

Dad, Agnes and Marjorie
Black Satin Coat and Bonnet

Sally, Willie, Isobel, Agnes and Marjorie

The Old Scrap Screen

The Black Patent Shoes

Father With His New Car
Bankfoot, 1927

Sally, Agnes and Marjorie
Cottage Garden

All of One Frosty Day

The Nesting Box

Mother's Herbarium

Mother's Herbarium

Sally, Mother and Isobel
Queensferry, August 1920

Auntie Jean
Mother's Sister, with Mary Jane

Naming the Moon for the Ox-eye Daisy

Mother in the Garden
Seton

These Were the Calendulas

Marjorie

arranged around the oval stone and strong curving claws, and it sets up all kinds of conjectures as to who had worn it last and how the wearer was finally parted from it.

I can only think of it as the owl which sat all of one frosty day in the apple tree and took wing silently and mysteriously towards evening when the winter sun resembled a great blood orange in the sky.

26

Seventh Daughter

Because I was the Seventh Daughter I was said to possess certain powers of healing. It boiled down to a Seventh Daughter having power to cure scrofula or what was known as King's Disease. Along with Kings then I had power to cure what sounded a rather unpleasant glandular complaint, but as I never knew or heard of anyone who suffered from it my powers in that direction remained untested.

It is true though that throughout my life I performed some very minor unimportant miracles.

The nesting box was hung against the wall of the house just outside my bedroom window. The entrance hole was too big for a tomtit or a wren but maybe the sparrow would make use of it.

By late May the sparrow had inspected it, found the box wanting and nested as usual under the eaves of the house. White summer jasmine clambered round the box and in July perfume from delicate tubular flowers would tantalise pale moths at evening.

Finally, after the box had been lined with dried bracken fronds, the robins chose to nest in it and long hours were spent watching their flightings to and fro, as regularly and surely as bees heading homewards from the heather beds. We forgot everything, housework, garden and necessary chores in this wonderful all-absorbing activity going on outside my bedroom window.

One morning, so early it was still dark, I was awakened by a stealthy movement outside. I sprang out of bed and without pausing to draw on dressing gown or slippers stood at the window listening. Stealthy groping sounds were followed by vague scufflings. Several times there was a short silence then gropings and scufflings started again.

I was not usually nervous although I slept downstairs with my window open but the unidentifiable sounds held me rooted to the spot. Suddenly my knees gave way as a shape, only one shade darker than the gloom outside, launched itself against the window. In the split second before giving way to utter fear the shape resolved itself into a cat and by the time I realised what it was doing in such a peculiar situation the creature had detached itself from the summer jasmine and disappeared. The stealthy sounds had been the animal groping to insert a paw into the nesting hole and then jostling for a firmer foothold on the creeper.

I went back to bed rather shakily. There was nothing to be done just then as it was still quite dark. I fell into an uneasy sleep and it was the keening of the robins that wakened me. Fetching a ladder in that queer half-light that precedes the dawn I climbed up and surveyed the dishevelled nest. Wisps of bracken waving in the dawn breeze were the only indication that it had been tampered with. Impossible to tell what damage had been done inside. One movement lifted the box off its hook.

In the scullery I wrenched the lid off the box. The Seventh Child had arrived on the scene and together we stared at the frail nest's pathetic contents – four tiny nestlings cold and quite dead. The cat's proddings had frightened the mother off and they had lain unprotected for hours.

I was quite positive afterwards that I didn't think of it myself. I simply moved as though bidden to do so and fetched the hot waterbottle with the lavender velvet cover. I heated water in the kettle and poured some into the bag and set it down on the copper. Without any hope at all, expecting nothing, the Seventh Child and I lifted the tiny cold bodies onto the waterbottle and straightened out each scrawny neck. I didn't know what to do next so we just stood there helpless. Then stared in disbelief.

I couldn't believe it. One nestling was palpitating slightly and suddenly it gaped. Two minute wings quite innocent of feathers fluttered feebly. The second little bird was coming to life and gradually all four were convulsed with movement.

This is what it must be like to be God, I thought. God the All Powerful, the Giver of Life.

In the hawthorn tree the parent birds were patiently waiting. It wasn't easy handling tiny quivering creatures that hadn't even strength enough to hold up their heads but with the Seventh Child's help I replaced them and tied the lid firmly on with string.

"We mustn't expect too much," I said. "The parents might desert." For we both knew wild things don't like to be interfered with and robins particularly like privacy.

With the box once more firmly in position we drew up chairs to the window, filled a hot waterbottle each, and sat down to sip warm milk and watch. Nothing happened for a long time and it was after a great many preliminaries that first one and then the other robin flew onto the box and peered in. Finally the female entered and stayed inside and from then on all went well.

Of course anyone could have done it – a simple case of resuscitation. There was nothing remarkable about it at all. Except that I hadn't thought about doing what I did. But then I had the power, you see, being a Seventh Daughter and having the power to cure scrofula.

Later I tested my powers further. I would lie in bed at night completely relaxed, shutting everything out so that my breathing almost stopped and nothing existed outside myself and no sounds or feelings came through to me at all. My eyes under closed lids turned further and further up and I seemed to leave my body there on the bed and go soaring up. And I took the person with me – the one I was praying for.

There was a radiance up there, far up through the darkness, and I had to reach it and enter it or at least touch it before I knew that everything was going to be all right and whoever I prayed for was going to get well.

Sometimes the radiance was in the shape of a cross and sometimes it was just like the hem of a garment, but if I reached it I had attained the ultimate and then I seemed to fall down through the darkness until I lay on my bed again exhausted and drew a deep breath and yawned and turned over and fell asleep. And the person would get well.

But sometimes although I tried for hours I couldn't do it. There was no radiance and the experience just wouldn't happen.

Perhaps it was all nonsense and they would have recovered anyway, but it was such a comfortable happy feeling up there and you were so sure everything would be all right it seemed to be worth the effort.

27

Limacidae

A scream from the Seventh Child summoned us all to the coal cellar where she had gone to shovel coal and there, fully extended to at least six inches, lay this fearsomely-horned reptilian looking creature as thick as a cat's paw and bearing the name of its species 'Limacidae'. I had nothing against the appellation which seems to suggest a smooth liquid gliding movement, and the creature does indeed try to bear it out by having nothing attached to its person such as legs or feet or joints or even sinews that might cause a jerk or a jolt in its efforts to get from here to yonder.

The cellar was one thing but when this naked mollusc decided to explore scullery and larder, penetrated a downstairs bedroom and was finally found exquisitely colour-blended and boiled in a pot of lentil soup, the hunt was on and Limacidae became one of the few creatures we decided must of necessity be destroyed.

Glistering shiny trails during damp weather led everywhere – to and from the cat's plate but the slug was not there; across a bedroom carpet and into a shoe cupboard but neither was the Limacidae there – at least not visibly until I thrust my foot into a bedroom slipper after which, although partly squashed, it extended horns and crawled off apparently unhurt. It seems that, like lizards, some molluscs when injured can grow new segments and even sever parts of a tail in order to make their escape.

There are reports of a "highly gifted young woman" who actually trained one of these slugs to come to her and it ignored all other voices and immediately began travelling in her direction.

But we kept none of them long enough to train and instead flushed them swiftly down the toilet. To turn them out of doors even in the hardest weather solved nothing for slugs have been frozen stiff for days and still return to life at a rise in temperature.

Some shell varieties which had been brought from Egypt were gummed on a sheet of paper and placed in a glass case in a museum and were found to be alive after a period of two years. They are even reputed to bite, the jaws rasping against your hand so that the part feels tender and smarting like a slight burn for days afterwards.

28

"A Bee is Little"

Bombus Terrestris. Bombus Terrestris. It had a sleepy soothing sound in keeping with the dizzy droning and incessant flight that went on all around us. For the bumblebees had lived for years under rotting floorboards in the outhouse and we had sat there for as long in striped deckchairs or white-painted Colonial chairs with delicately woven backs and platforms to support the feet and never once had those heavy creatures, the huge bull-tailed bumblebees, collided with any of us as they zoomed homewards laden with honey or eagerly quested outwards.

Occasionally a casualty had to be lifted from the ground and with a skilful flick of the wrist, set on the wing again. And never in all that time had any of us been stung although I suppose the Bombus Terrestris does sting sometimes if you make it mad enough.

They had their drones too – great bumbling fellows barred from the hive that sheltered them warm and fed them fat with sugar. They trailed velvet bodies around on the earth's surface, too lazy to raise wings in flight. So from lack of usage, the wings wither and shrink and they lose altogether the power of flight and remain earthbound until, soaked by showers that refresh the night they can no longer climb the antirrhinum stem to dip curving antennae deep in the sweetness of the nectar there and so they die, lying on their backs with little spurred legs spread heavenward in an agony of supplication.

We knew all about the little honey pot the bee had built under the rotting wood at the entrance to her nest and the eggs and the grubs and the young worker bees that would eventually make their appearance.

Bee stings are good for rheumatism so they say but, anyway, we knew that if a bee did sting the last thing to do was shake it off. For if you have the courage of endurance and can bear the pain a while the bee will work his body carefully round and round about until the sting is extracted. Make friends with pain and the sting will ease your rheumatism. But if you brush the bee off roughly the sting will remain under the skin and cause a lot of trouble – and the bee will die which seems a pity.

So we respected the Bombus Terrestris and they continued to thrive all through the summer even when the outhouse door was shut and they had to find their way through the chinks of the wall or underneath the badly fitting door, and in winter they lay asleep under rotting floorboards.

We loved them for being part of the summer scene; for hovering over spikes of lavender in company with honey bees and earth bees, vestal cuckoo bees and small red-glowing velvet bees that might be called by another name just as improbable. Part of the activity that never ceased, they bumbled lightly past us on the outward journey and, heavily laden, homeward with the baskets on their legs brimful with honey.

You would have been sorry to have stolen that honey and to have eaten it for you felt about them as you had felt about the bumblebees that bumbled all night long above the old box bed at the cottage.

"A bee is little among such as fly but her fruit is the chief of sweet things."

29

Spring Tonic

The child was not my child of course but she came with her mother, Mary Kelly, to the house when she was three because she was too young to be at school and because she would be no trouble.

I liked to think that the child and I were friends as she trotted along at my side on short tartan-clad legs. She had few words, although with her mother she could sustain some animated conversation. With you it was generally a nod or a shake of the head but she was, as the mother had said, "no trouble". Absolutely no trouble at all, never cross, never crying and seldom out of sorts but when she was the eyes grew darker and the small face flushed and a thumb was thrust into a drooping mouth, but no complaint ever uttered. Her most emphatic statement was made when one of us hunted unsuccessfully for a biscuit tin which, with her small stature, she could see easily on the shelf below. Exasperated at last to something like fury she burst out, "It's *oonder!*"

In winter our kitchen was warm and fragrant with floury baking smells. The child's mother is flour to the elbows as she stoops over the fire swaddling fragile triangles – oatcakes in a spotless napkin.

The edges of the triangles curl delicately like rose petals in the sun or the lily hands of Indian dancers.

Offer her a chair and she will say "That'll mak' a differ," and calls you something that sounds like a "peedie badoo" which in her native Orkney means "a nice little girl". Great paddy flakes drift past the window and the oatcakes are delicious eaten hot and dripping with butter.

And the pancakes! The round black girdle shows no apparent heat till lightly smeared with golden fat which sizzles and bubbles at the contact. Gently the delicious mixture, dropped from a spoon's tip, spreads slowly at first like a small sea of lava suddenly arrested by the heat to throw up bubbles that deflate to form tiny encrustations upon a moon's face. The knife blade is thrust beneath the small mass and skilfully turned. Displaying a gently browned surface the semi-solid grips iron, begins mysteriously to rise. Again at the right moment the steel blade flicks and there emerges perfectly cooked, a pancake!

We went through sometimes to watch the baking and mother would speak about recipes and could never give exact quantities partly because she knew it all without thinking, partly because she never had time to consult recipe books. It was all in her head anyway and you could never pin her down to exactitudes.

One concoction she made up every spring, like some kind of ritual, – and I remember her doing it when I was quite a little thing – was the spring medicine guaranteed to clear the blood and give you a beautiful skin. The mixture was made up in a tall wine bottle and the cloudy liquid was shaken up every morning and she and the girls of the family drank from a stemless wine glass. "A teaspoonful of Epsom Salts, a teaspoonful of Cream of Tartar, a teaspoonful of Salts of . . . " But obliterated from my memory is the final vital ingredient. Salts of what? Always as a child I persisted in saying "Salts of Sorrel" and as this invariably raised a laugh I kept on saying it so that now I cannot for the life of me imagine what the salts might have been.

It's like mispronouncing a word for fun and always afterwards you hesitate and have to think twice. It worked though – the spring medicine – and I remember Mary once saying to me "What have you done to your skin?" and I never wanted to miss the magic potion after that.

30

Mother's Book

Mother was brought up on Bible tracts and religious publications for children and she could remember grandfather, who had a deep stentorian voice, repeating a grace "as long as your arm" so that food was always cold but had to be eaten because grandmother would have nothing wasted.

As a Christmas present grandfather gave her a reading book inscribed "For Eva – a present from her Father – 25th December 1878. May thy Christmas be happy."

The book was published with a view to filling a want "often felt by those who have the charge of the education of Girls, by supplying a connecting link between the mental training they receive at school and the practical duties of a woman's life."

In the first chapter the meaning of Domestic Economy is made quite clear by the simple expedient of applying the word domestic to the cat – 'a cat is a *domestic* animal.' Then Phoebe, who is a year or two older, exclaims that economy must mean saving money, for their mother often says she must "practise great economy" and therefore cannot afford to buy things which can be done without.

Mother was so glad for instance to be able to spend sixpence a yard instead of fivepence on print for the girls' summer dresses. So the little girls arrive at the conclusion that "Domestic Economy" means the "right management of a house".

A girl must know her duty to her parents and not make mother's heart heavy with anxiety by being a foolish undutiful child but rather learn to make father glad.

Evidently the Edinburgh climate does not alter much with the passing years for Eva is advised "in a changeable climate like ours", to wear a woollen garment to protect the chest and lungs. The ideal material suggested for this knitted vest is soft wool at threepence halfpenny or fourpence halfpenny an ounce, but a cheaper yarn will do "to which the skin will become accustomed although it may seem a little rough at first." Red flannel for a bodice and petticoat are also recommended which sounds cheerfully cosy.

"How nice it is," says the book, "to have a pretty bonnet and right and natural that a girl should wish for one, but it would be poor comfort to reflect that there was a new bonnet on her head if in the depth of winter she was shivering for want of a flannel petticoat." Neat underwear was a sign of true womanly refinement whether in sight or out of it.

The two important rules to apply to dress were neatness and suitability particularly when choosing a Sunday dress – suitability to the wearer's purse, her station, age, figure, complexion and to the time of the year.

"Did the reader ever go to a school treat in tight boots?" Then she has already learned that even a little pain can mar a great deal of pleasure. Eva is instructed how to ensure good health with the help of three principal factors – Good Air, Good Water and Good Food.

In a chapter on food she is told what people eat in India and why the people of Greenland subsist almost entirely on fish. There is only one kind of food which contains everything the human body needs, says the book, and that is milk. "Little babies ought to have nothing else until they are a twelvemonth old. The poor little creatures cannot digest any other kind of food." What would they think of the stout, robust occupants of today's perambulators and the hearty meal of solids tackled by a modern baby of seven months or even earlier?

There is a neat little food-table given with a carefully tabulated list of Body-Warmers and Flesh-Formers.

"What is soup made of?" was apparently a favourite question in school. On one occasion only one little girl ventured the answer "of a neck of mutton". Of course, agrees the book, excellent soup can be made from a neck of mutton but there are many less expensive ways – a sheep's head, an oxcheek or a shin of beef or even vegetables alone make nourishing soups.

Mastication is dealt with in detail. The teeth are for biting, tearing and grinding and the child had to have a pretty good idea of the function of her stomach and how food is digested. Besides learning the duties of a nurse she is instructed how to apply a tourniquet and thus avert death from bleeding.

All the lessons are illustrated by incidents from history or literature. The story of King Lear and his daughters points the moral in Duty to Parents. The Black Hole of Calcutta emphasises the need for fresh air. The volume is interspersed with poetry – 'The Cotter's Saturday Night', Wordsworth's 'Skylark', 'The Living Temple' by O.W. Holmes and others.

The Victorian child knew all about Galileo discovering that the earth moves round the sun and how Dr Harvey discovered the circulation of the blood. Indeed she herself was well acquainted with how the blood circulates through the body.

"Praised be the Lord for our sister water who is very useful to us, and humble, and precious and clean!" sang St Francis of Assisi, and so Eva learned how indispensable water is for drinking and washing, that lack of cleanliness and bad housing resulted in the

Plague and how this calamity was followed up by the Great Fire of London.

At the end there is a calculation of weekly earnings and expenditure taken from Mrs Beeton's Penny Cookery Book. Where the weekly earnings are 10/-, Daily Expenditure on food may be 10d, Weekly Expenditure on Ditto. - 5/10d, and Reserve for Rent, Clothes &c. 4/2d. There is a note appended here – "I think we must suppose that the cost of fuel will be included under the head of Weekly Expenditure on Food, i.e. 5/10d."

An inspiring and very sound little book. It is small wonder that a generation brought up on it possessed backbone and the determination to tackle anything from cheerfully bringing up thirteen children in a three-roomed cottage to cooking a meal for eight persons on a close range or "kitchener" costing from 28/- to 35/-.

"Whatsoever thy hand findeth to do, do it with all thy might."

What a solemn little mite an eight-year-old sounds getting out for church and Sunday School three times on the Sabbath and in between sitting behind closely-drawn blinds reading her Bible or digesting that much prized gift from her father – her reading book.

31

Once in a Blue Moon

"Once in a blue moon" but one can recall nothing spectacular or outstanding happening except the blue moon itself and to make it even stranger, the blue sun. Of course the moon shines with the reflected light of the sun so it was not to be wondered at that the moon should be blue if the sun was.

I was light-headed with it calling the attention of passers-by to this perhaps once-in-a-lifetime phenomenon. What if they missed it? For there it was, a blue orb glaring like some Cyclopean eye from an unremarkable colourless firmament.

But by the time night had come the blue moon seemed so much more beautiful and obvious than a blue sun had been. Besides, now telephones and televisions and radios had spread the news and everybody was ready for it and there was no need for me to spread the moonshine further.

I couldn't stop looking at it, the sun by day or the moon by night. They held me riveted and unable to remove my gaze in case that small steel-blue disc should disappear behind a cloud or vanish altogether.

A cloud of red dust blown all the way down from the Arizona Desert, they explained, as if I wanted to hear their dull prosaic scientific explanation any more than I wanted to know that the moon itself was a cold burnt-out planet covered with volcanic scars and craters and that moon dust, should I ever see a handful, was grey and uninspiring and as painful as a penance.

Rather I wanted to go on believing in the moon as the mirror of the sun which it is, this satellite of earth casting moonglades on the water, naming the moonflower for the ox-eye daisy and casting moonbows and rings around the moon so that there would be a wedding soon.

You felt no gratitude to astronauts for making your moonshiny dreams unreal. Rather would you have held the vision of a moon beaming tranquilly down upon an earth asleep, shining silver and casting deeper shadows than the sun himself.

Once in a blue moon. It can only happen once. A second coming would be infinitely undesirable.

32

Squirrels in Winter Woods

It was as though the war years had never been. The excitement, the fear, the tears and anxieties were all over and I came home to find mother ill.

The Seventh Child wanted to but finally *I* stayed because she had a remunerative job and I would have to look around and so it came about that for the next twenty years I was to live a kind of Count of Monte Cristo existence – not that I dug tunnels or scrabbled out holes for escape. In my own particular way I was happy. It was as though I renounced life willingly and found a kingdom here whose boundaries were the house and the walls of the garden. It was as though I had been drowning and all of a sudden had given up struggling.

And in this new kingdom mother was the only one who really mattered. The whole house started to revolve around her and her alone, and her bedroom was the hub so that there was a worn trail on the green carpet like a path straggling through woods.

Sometimes she was well and appeared in the doorway with her arms full of flowers – poppies and monkshood and great horse-daisies –

"Oh, the darlings!" and at other times we almost lost her – so often in fact that we began to lose count of the times and then we tiptoed about the house, ate meals in silence and stood at her bedroom door listening and counting the barely perceptible breathing. And sometimes when we had given up hope she would suddenly rally and open her eyes and hiss weakly "Shut that door!" and we laughed with relief and ran for warm milk and glucose and whisky.

Sometimes I stood in the garden listening to life and the world going by outside and about me: the sound of traffic, voices and laughter. So that sometimes I felt desolate.

In March the sun could shine with summer heat bringing out crowds of drowsy bees to visit modest clumps of city snowdrops or rest against white-painted ferns of garden seats.

Pussywillows grown tall from a rooted cutting lost their first silvered flush, and fat now with sleek grey fur awaited another day's sun to turn them into pollen balls of golden yellow soon to be thick with hovering bees. Winter jasmine, no longer bound in sarcophagus of ice, covered grey walls with a galaxy of yellow stars.

> I knew that the spring had come
> Not because of the bees in the willow trees
> But because there were whips and tops
> In the two little village shops.

But the day she died was not like that.

I had known when Mary brought the red and white flowers and I arranged them in a jug and carried them into the bedroom that this was the end – inevitably, inexorably. There was nothing I could do to prevent it.

When she was dying we fed squirrels in winter woods. How could we? Yet there was pleasure in it still, the heart turning away from unhappiness and pain like a flower wanting to turn towards the light. And rejection of the truth of course for we didn't want to accept that.

I asked, "Can't you tell me what's wrong? Please can't you speak?" And she opened her lips to answer, thought better of it then shook her head and turned away.

"You do believe that we'll all meet again though, don't you?" I had persisted earlier. "I don't know. I really don't know." The whisper shocked more than I could have believed for she had always gone to church – had loved going to church. Her life was a dedication to others and if she wasn't sure then who in the world could be?

She died when it was winter – a winter lasting into spring when early flowerings were caught and held fast in frozen earth as animals are caught in traps.

And three days later when we buried her the whole world trembled into life – a day of sunlight and birdsong and warmth and bees hovered round the cortège trying to get through to the mound of flowers – her flowers, her darlings. As though all the things she had loved welcomed her to them and the earth was warm and shimmering in an ecstasy to receive her back.

Then winter settled in again and I froze into myself like a snail sealed against the windowpane. The house was my shell and I withdrew into it much as I had during the last twenty years but then I had an object. Now there was noone and the shell of the house fitted only me.

33

Golden Calendulas

My affinity lay with the golden flowers – the coltsfoot, the celandines, the dent-de-lion or lion's tooth, the sun spurge that turns its flowers to the sun, sunflowers and marigolds; all warm and ray-floreted, rich-glowing like the sun himself, shaggy and sweet, dizzying with their scent of pollen bees so lately roused from dormancy of winter sleep.

Especially the marigolds which the Virgin wore in her bosom so it is said, the luminous calendulas, shining with particular brilliance like lesser suns by day and still glimmering in the halflight of evening. For I had always accepted the almost physical excitement with which marigolds affect me by day when they exude their odour of such peculiar pungency.

Until one very dark night I, always a restless sleeper, stood at the window shortly after midnight staring out at the extinguished garden. Not quite extinguished though for my eyes, gradually becoming accustomed to the darkness, noticed a triangular-shaped area of light in one of the flowerbeds. Light shining through the french window can shed itself in a beam like a miniature searchlight straight up the garden path – just missing the flowerbed though. Besides, the study was in darkness.

I tried averting my gaze from the flowerbed but on returning to the area found the glow even more pronounced and one large bloom, taller than the others and dominating the triangle, shone apart from the mass with a stronger light. These were the calendulas, marigolds gleaming self-luminous in the darkness snuffing out pale wavering flames of iceland poppies.

These were my darlings then – flowers that pulsated with and radiated light by day and by night and not only their petals but also the foliage. The naturalists knew of it of course and it was galling to have to share knowledge of the phenomenon. I could have wished it to be my secret alone. "The appearance of the luminous vapour," one wrote, "floating over the leaf's surface (like moonlight over rippling water) was strikingly beautiful." It was and I had to agree with their accounts of mimic lightning playing over the petals in a kind of pulsing phosphorescence. Coleridge expresses it most perfectly:

'Tis said at summer's evening hour,
Flashes the golden-coloured flower,
A fair electric flame.

Even so a group of coltsfoot raised on jointed stems and pressing ardently upwards from a heap of shale or rubble by the wayside had me on my knees. Solar, solstice, solarium – these were my words. Ra, Mithras and Apollo – all these were my names just as the Sunbear, the Sunbird, the Sun Bittern and the Sun Fish were my creatures living and delighting in rays from that central body of the solar system around which planets revolve in their orbits and from which their light and heat is derived.

The sun is the key and the atmosphere the keyhole. And the sun must penetrate the atmosphere – to fit into the keyhole so that it can provide us with that heat we need to make things grow – to make us grow.

I was nearer the sun in Greece and drowned in it in Delphi. In Delphi I was submerged in a golden brazen burnished sea of sun. Delphi the centre of the world cradled by the twin Phaedriades – the Shining Rocks – the Rhodini and the Phleboukos, rocks that gather the sunlight to themselves and reflect it back pink and golden and shining.

In golden Mycenae, treasure house of priceless metals beaten to shape masks to transform indifferent human features; to deck heaving female bosoms with bee ornaments clasping a ball of honey; to scatter grave clothes with golden stars; to coil rings for ladies' fingers. The guide entreats earnestly to show me the Secret Cistern. But who desires the damp darkness of Pluto's underworld when here above ground is the very source of the treasure of life itself? The sun which in northern climes radiates through cloud, through smoke, through smog like the spokes of some gigantic wheel. The wheel of the sun turning, ever turning on its eternal hub. Sun and planet geared so that one wheel moves around another.

But here in Mycenae shining on beehive tombs, on shaft graves and grave circles pilloried of wealth and human remains long since mouldered into dust, it heralds the way up a country road lined with oleanders, up the cruel and stony pathway through the Lion Gate and into the Golden Age.

The sun can blind as it blinded the master of San Michèle. Or it can prolong contemplation of so much beauty that destroyed his sight much as small boys spike the eyes of sparrows and finches and hang the tiny quivering creatures jerking like puppets from a string.

Was that what blinded me then? Contemplation of too much beauty? For beauty could hurt me like a knife-thrust in the heart. "Look not upon me because I am black," sang Solomon, "because the sun hath looked upon me." But I am not black although the

119

sun has looked upon me many times where I sit at the feet of the Great Bear.

We stepped together into the El Dorado of the woods, I and the labrador with his great heavy pads and tail turning in delight like a tawny handle. It was like stepping into a world of light through a shower of leonids or falling trinkets, through a munificence of winged discs some round or shaped like digits or delicately notched by some finer cutting edge than steel.

All through that afternoon the winged gold ends fell thickly, settling around us on the ground like coins spilled from some aerial treasure trove. They fell and lay weightless on the ground.

What could I say about this autumn afternoon that could please me? That had not been said before?

"Margaret are you grieving?"

I said nothing that the dog could not have said with his eyes a thousand times better.

I am the symbol of the sun – a circle with a dot in the middle. I am the centre but the circle keeps me in and prevents others entering. I am Leonardo's naked man – the man within a sphere. Always the barrier permanent and insurmountable.

I had always noticed how the further away two points recede the closer they become, whether horizontal or perpendicular, or curving to the left or to the right. Am I the obstacle that prevents the merging and the flowing together of all kinds of situations and people and objects? They call it perspective and they may be right.

But I sit there between the pillars of the fireplace and the pillars are wider apart at the base and I, sitting here in the middle, force them apart by my very being, with the fact of my existence. Yet as soon as they get slightly above and beyond me they begin almost imperceptibly to come together, to converge.

Today, sitting in the Reference Library, I look back from some incredible distance. These young people incite me to worse extravagances of despair. That small chubby child there, twelve years at most, handles great tomes with ease. Adroitly he manipulates his ruler to draw a definitive line – there. A finishing line or a beginning? Who is to know? His looseleaf notebook is neatly anotated, neatly ruled, meticulously illustrated. As he goes on he becomes more flushed, rosebud lips part further, the work mounts beneath his childish dimpled hand.

Today I have a headache. The same headache I had yesterday and the day before and the day before that. Nothing is finished. Nothing ever will be finished now.

Skies are overcast, sufficiently overcast to obscure the sun and the blue infinity. Yet somewhere up there the sun in shining. Up there where, at their perspective game again, the pillars seem to meet. Do they meet?

And so I have a headache. Because the sky is obscuring the sun.

All my life I have felt it – an ebb and flow of the tide towards and away from people. Sometimes I am swept very close but so seldom close enough. Often another larger wave carries me away completely and I never make up the leeway. Again carried off to a certain distance I wallow there, waiting it seems for a stronger surge to sweep me back – to make up the ground I have lost. Sometimes I cry out "Hurry, come and get me or I'll be carried too far, far away beyond all reach." And sometimes it happens and I'm lost and I have lost you too. Completely, utterly. Knowing that we can never meet again.

The same thing happens to a lesser degree with people who don't count so much; those who surge in and out and into our lives again never meaning very much but necessary to the pattern of the moment.

For life is like a carpet and, like a carpet, runs in safe, familiar patterns but only for so long. Then suddenly the pattern is discontinued. Never mind, we pick up a new thread and weave our way along it like gigantic spiders climbing up or falling down, shaken by the wind of change, broken sometimes, meeting happiness sometimes. Then the pattern steadies itself and on we go again until it becomes familiar and known and safe. Until the pattern is discontinued once more.

34

Mirror, Mirror on the Wall

And so the twenty incredible years passed filled with such endless variety, with such discoveries. A friend once asked what did I do with my time and I hesitated and answered, I really don't think you would understand. Could I begin to explain how my life was filled with the contemplation of simple things, having her to care for, she of the herbarium and the Reading Book and the poppies?

Now I walk winter, spring or summer woods with the dog who swings his tail like a tawny handle and turns swiftly at every corner to look back. To ascertain what? I am not the one he looks for so earnestly. For Mary has gone now and for a while he lingers here with me in the present because the woods are alive with her presence and the river which mirrors beech and hornbeam and mallard so faithfully also holds her laughing face leaning over the copingstone of some ancient bridge.

Dreams bring them all back again of course. I can awaken from a dream as from another life so vividly real that it is difficult to get back into the present and the sense of having been with someone is so powerful that the presence sustains me all day long although retreating as the day wears on, gently shaking me off to return to some shadowy other world where I have no place.

It is as though they are all there behind the old scrap screen staring down through the eyes of Gladstone or Parnell and a voice calls softly through the night, "She'll be all right, Muma, she's not fevered." And the person with the voice pushes a rice biscuit into your hand and kisses you and turns away into the shadows.

Still the square remains, the barriers impenetrable. Still the dot is in the circle and the naked man in the centre of a sphere and I am sitting here forcing the pillars apart with my very being.

And what of Honi Soit. . .?
Mirror, mirror on the wall. Honi Soit Qui Mal y Pense. Shame on him who thinks evil of it.